W9-DHS-316

A Party Begins in the Heart

A Party
Begins
in the *Heart*

Sue Buchanan

WORD PUBLISHING
NASHVILLE
A Thomas Nelson Company

Published by Word Publishing, a unit of Thomas Nelson, Inc.,
P.O. Box 141000, Nashville, Tennessee 37214

Copyright © 2001 by Sue Buchanan. All rights reserved.

No portion of this book may be reproduced, stored in a retrieval system, or
transmitted in any form or by any means—electronic, mechanical, photocopy,
recording, or any other—except for brief quotations in printed reviews, without
the prior permission of the publisher.

ISBN 0-8499-1688-7

Library of Congress Cataloging-in-Publication Data available

Printed in the United States of America
01 02 03 04 05 06 BVG 9 8 7 6 5 4 3 2 1

Contents

Section One:

Section Two:

Section Five:

Introduction

I'm writing this book because if there is one thing I know, it's how to celebrate! I wasn't necessarily born with the gift, but I'm a fast learner; I've found out *you hang out with people you want to be like*. Hopefully some of the good stuff will rub off. Many of the people I admire are normal, everyday, friends and family. My husband, for instance. If you've read my book *I'm Alive and the Doctor's Dead*, you know that when it comes to Christmas, Wayne's middle name is *Celebrate*. If you missed the story, I've included it in the *Celebrating the Occasion* section.

Some of the people I want to be like and have had the privilege of hanging out with are celebrity-types like Liz Curtis Higgs, Dianna and Jerry Jenkins, Vestal Goodman, Joni Eareckson Tada, Sheila Walsh, Bill and Gloria Gaither, Mark Lowry, Sandi Patty, and others. Can you believe that when I asked the question "Can I write about you?" not one person said "No"? This, in spite of the fact they know I'm a regular Liz Smith for believers—an *enquiring-minds-wanna-know* type gal. My spiritual gift is *exaggeration!*

Even when I explained right up front that this book would be kinda *gossipy* (in the best sense of the word, of course), each person, seemingly without a second thought, said "Yes, write anything you want about me." Knowing me, I wouldn't have said that; but now that I know they trust me, I'll be forced to stay as close to the truth as possible.

Between the stories, you'll find joyful little tips for creating *a party in the heart* lifestyle, songs to sing, and some recipes! Why recipes you ask? Well, duh! How can you celebrate without food?

The Scripture that is scattered throughout is only to be used in an emergency when you are feeling brain dead—when your prayers don't seem to be getting any higher than the ceiling fan. When your heart has *done run out of party!* God has given us the opportunity to put His very own words in our mouths. He knew *there would be days like this!* Feel free to shout these verses aloud whenever! Wherever! Feel free to call me when you get arrested for disturbing the peace. My machine will be on!

Introductions by My Daughters

From Mindy

My mother is one of the most beautifully unpredictable characters you'll ever meet! She possesses the unique gift of finding a way to make even your darkest moments seem brighter and more bearable.

She takes great pride in giving you frivolous—even silly!—gifts to inspire a smile! My most recent present from her was a pink frog from a trip of hers to New Orleans. I always wanted a pink frog!

She could also be deemed *the queen of clever comebacks.* You have to stay on your toes just to have a conversation with her! In spite of herself, she has taught me one of the most valuable lessons in my life—that above all else we need to love and be loved! We need to cherish the friendships that God puts in our lives, and most of all have as much fun as possible doing it.

Melinda Sue Buchanan

From Dana

I can't tell you how many times I've heard it. After people have spent any length of time at all with my mother, they tell me: "Ooooh, your mother is so much fun! It must be sooo fun having her around all the time! I'd just looove having her as *my* mother!"

Really? Put yourself in my shoes for a minute. Imagine that you're a professional harpist (which I am), entertaining at a very *elegant* and *tasteful* Christmas party. As you are playing, your mother—whom you didn't expect to see at this gathering of people you are dying to impress—waltzes in the door with a "Hey, everybody, here I am!" expression on her party-girl face.

Trying your best to keep *Chestnuts Roasting on an Open Fire* going with one hand as you cover your mouth with the other, you look her up and down. Then it strikes you: She's wearing a glittery bustier—with at least an inch of midriff showing! (For those of you who don't know what a "bustier" is since the godly women in your circles don't wear them, *think Madonna!*)

Horrified you try to slink beneath the harp—a trick that rarely works. "Why can't she be like all the other mothers?" you think for the thousandth time. But at the very same moment, the crowd erupts in cheers! After all, a party is underway—and the life of the party has just arrived!

When your mother is the ultimate party girl, anything—and I mean *anything*—can happen. For example, there was the time when my church was planning a women's conference, and one of the ladies piped up: "Isn't *your mother* a speaker?" Calculating the risks—my husband was an associate pastor at the time—I breathed a timid, "Yes, but . . ."

Next thing I knew, I was standing in a church bathroom with my mother. We were on a five-minute countdown to the start of the conference. But Mother wasn't dressed in the lovely silk suit I'd pictured her wearing—nor was she going over the godly words of wisdom I'd hoped she'd share with the ladies. (She does have some—godly wisdom—you know!)

Instead, she was jerking on her Edna Puckett get-up. "Aunt Edna" is Mother's alter-ego. She wears a curly gray wig, smeared lipstick, saggy panty-hose, and some even saggier body parts. Edna is the persona Mother assumes when she wants to say anything she wants—and get away with it scot-free! Her plan was to make a grand entrance as Edna Puckett, then spend the next few minutes poking irreverent fun at the senior pastor . . . the music director . . . and *me!*

"Mother," I gasped, "you don't dare!"

She dared.

Long story short, by the next day Barry and I could have been looking for another church—in another denomination, in another state! Unbelievably, we weren't. The ladies loved her. They ate up her Edna shtick—*and* the wisdom she later shared—with a fork and spoon. And an ordinary women's conference became a celebration. A party, if you will! Eventually, even I came out of my fetal position and enjoyed the evening—still vowing I'd never let her embarrass me again. Too late! She's publishing another book!

There's one more thing you should know about Mother. Some moms collect little figurines and tchotchkes they keep in curio cabinets. But my mother collects *friends*. And you too will become her friend as you read this book. She'll teach you to celebrate and party with the best of them—even if you, like me, wouldn't be caught dead in a bustier!

Dana (Buchanan) Shafer

Author's note: It was *not* a bustier! Bustiers look like fancy push-up bras. "Push-up" is synonymous with "cleavage!" What I was wearing was a gold-ish, sequin-ish, halter-ish thing, with a black satin jacket over it, for heaven's sake! Tasteful-ish, actually. You couldn't see a thing, much less two inches of midriff—*where does she come up with this stuff? A glimpse* at the very most!

Section One

Celebrating the People, the Music, and the Words!

Every life has its turning points, those few times in one's existence when something happens that is so profound life is never again the same. Moments like getting married and having children. And making a decision to follow Christ, that's a real life-changer! I did that when I was twelve years old. Now, I think becoming a Christian is a little like making a business decision. You weigh life with Christ; you weigh life without Christ. And duh! It's easy! A Christian not only has the assurance of going to heaven when life is over, but there are perks for daily living through the unlimited resources of the Holy Spirit. And think of the friends you meet!

The friends my husband and I met when we moved to Nashville over thirty years ago (another of my watershed moments) included musicians, songwriters, recording artists, music business gurus, publishers, authors, and *friends* of all the above! Our paradigm expanded in new and exciting ways, because of Wayne's job as marketing director at Benson Publishing Company. We found ourselves in the middle of this community of talented people that had one thing in mind: communicating the Christian message. As technology evolved, so did we. Some of us branched out into marketing, graphic art, studios, production, and all manner of support for this burgeoning industry.

The first two chapters in *Celebrating the Friends, the Music, and the Words!* will give you a pretty good picture of what it was like in those early days in Nashville. All the stories in this section are about people we knew then and still have as friends today. Gloria Gaither has become one of my very best friends as well as a writing partner (along with Joy MacKenzie and Peggy Benson) in two books, *Friends Through Thick and Thin* and *Confessions of Friends Through Thick and Thin*. Tanya Goodman Sykes we knew in those days as "Rusty's little girl." Today we know her as a professional musician and songwriter.

Many years later I had a turning point in my life of more profundity than I could have imagined. I had breast cancer, accompanied by a doom-and-gloom prognosis. Heretofore, I'd been one of those production people, a video and show producer. Cancer changed my life, and God somehow decided my message of hope and survival would be a good thing for others to hear—thus the books. And he knew I had good connections! Friends who were, and are, my champions! The connectivity in the family of God is the most amazing thing; we are truly one big family. Any story I might tell, any book I might write, if nothing else, is about my *friends*.

Chapter One

Go Back to Mars If You Aren't Up-to-Date on Gospel Music

To acknowledge the fact you've never heard of the Gaither Homecoming music videos, never caught so much as a glimpse of one of these musical extravaganzas on TV, would be like saying you've never heard of the White House! The Golden Gate Bridge! The Tower of London!

To say you haven't been totally caught up in the *joie de vivre* of the music and the camaraderie of the musicians, is like saying you can hold yourself back from saluting the flag at a football game!

And to admit you haven't fallen madly in love with this collection of unlikely characters—a cast of thousands who are much too happy for their own good—is like saying you don't love your mama.

If you are the one person left on the planet (perhaps you've been on a space mission to Mars) who has missed seeing these Homecoming videos, surf the channels practically any night of the week, and you can't miss 'em—this joyful (yes, rowdy) gang of singers, huggers, smilers, and sometimes, even criers.

"Have a Little Talk with Jesus," they're effusing with the greatest of gusto, as though they'd just come from an audience with the man himself! "In the Sweet By and Bye," they harmonize with seemingly more musical parts than you believed were vocally possible. High and low soprano. Alto? Two of those too! Tenor—as in *Myrtle, did you hear that?* And bass that, like the Energizer bunny, just keeps on going (lower and lower) long after, by all reasonable accounts, the notes should have run out.

These are songs you haven't heard since you were a child, sitting on your grandma's lap in the "Little Brown Church in the Wildwood," and yet surprise, surprise, they're relevant today! Right now . . . something tells me this music will outlive us all. Someday our children's children will be listening to it and watching these concerts by means of a chip in their thumbnail!

Even if you've never heard a gospel song in your life—even if God has done you wrong and you aren't on speaking terms with Him, for heaven's sake—you just can't help yourself! You gotta stayed tuned. Pretty soon you're tapping your toe and humming along. Next thing you know, you feel like you're right in the middle of a party! You're on a first-name basis with Vestal and Mark and the Martins. And even Bill and Gloria! Before you know it, you're calling the eight-hundred number (fully expecting Bill to answer the phone) and ordering the special deal of the moment.

For those of us who did attend that Little Brown Church in the Wildwood, we know that gospel music—and gospel singers— weren't always so sophisticated, so *uptown*. In fact, some of us knew it when it was a long-far-piece from no town in sight.

If a church in the wildwood isn't part of your past, and you wonder where this colorful form of music came from, perhaps the very best history lesson comes from a stage play—a spoof comedy—called *Smoke on the Mountain*.

The story opens inside a small rural church where the minister, a nervous-pervous-type guy with every preacher-ish mannerism you've ever seen and then some, has arrived ahead of time to prepare for the service. His grin is so fake and his behavior so overdramatized, you find yourself laughing right off the bat as he prances around flipping imaginary dirt from here and there with his big, white handkerchief, straightening song books and chairs along the way.

Next he stands behind the pulpit and practices—no audience, mind you! Leaning on the pulpit; *not* leaning on the pulpit; hands in an attitude of prayer; hands *waving* in the air. Open Bible; *closed* Bible; *Bible waving in the air!* He clears his throat. He straightens his bow tie. He whips out a pocket comb (the first of many times throughout the evening), and with herky-jerky (and hilariously funny) motions, rakes it over his head, all the while flashing his much-too-toothy smile at his imaginary audience. If that weren't enough, he resorts to the old spit-on-the-finger method to smooth his stubborn cowlick.

Then it's on to facial expressions. He tries them all, from an ear-to-ear grin that says, *Welcome! Glad ta have ya,* to a bull-dog-wrinkled, face-askew scowl that fairly shouts, *Come to Jesus or you'll burn in the lake of fire for all eternity!* The Bible never stops waving. In the middle of his charade—like he was caught in a freeze-frame—in walk the guest singers, the Sanders Family.

The group is made up of a controlling father, his moonshine nippin', just-out-of-prison brother, a Bible-quotin' wife, a pair of disgustingly cute, talented teen-age twins (boy and girl), and a rather pitiful second daughter who can't sing a lick. Her talents seems to be twofold: signing for the deaf and playing the tambourine. There's not a deaf person in sight and none are expected, but by George, that's her gift! As to playing the tambourine—loudly, with much fumbling and rarely on the beat—she's on a mission, an overly-dramatic and hilarious mission. *She will serve God with her gifts, or else!*

As the evening progresses, it becomes evident by the preacher's demeanor that things have gotten quite out of hand. He has to stop things and apologize often to the audience. The music is much too wild, the percussion instruments are totally unacceptable, and the singers entirely too unruly! He relaxes for a brief moment, however, when the music winds down and the performers begin to testify. Then horror of horrors, even their testimonies spell trouble!

They share their foibles and failures, describe in great detail the sins they've committed, and speculate about the lusts and desires of the flesh, making them sound quite appealing. The Sanders Family has glaring imperfections, but they don't let it get in the way of serving God. (At this point in the play, I'm remembering the times—during what was supposed to be a concert, yet the performer insisted on waxing eloquent—I've had the urge yell, "Shut up and sing!" Have you ever wondered, dear reader, why singers want to preach and preachers want to sing?)

When the Sanders begin their music again, *relief* is written on the reverend's face, and as the music becomes more raucous (Sister No-Talent is going a little crazy on the cymbals!), he begins to really get into it, clapping with gusto.

"Maybe God does approve of clapping," he admits tenuously, ". . . at least on Saturday nights."

Soon he's flirting with Sister No-Talent, picking up a tambourine of his own, and dancing a jig so raucous he knocks over the communion table.

"Does Jesus mind if a song has a little swing to it?" he asks, the fear of God written all over his rubbery face. Then, somehow gaining a little bravery, he smiles his most obnoxious and self-confident smile and adds, "I think He'd be right open-minded about it."

Thankfully, we are no longer spending precious time fighting battles over whether or not God approves. The bottom line is that we not allow the message to be compromised. Gospel music has become something of a phenomenon, and lives are being changed because of it.

As for the Homecoming videos, sales are staggering—in the millions—having out-sold such acts as Shania Twain, Ricky Martin, and the Backstreet Boys! There have been at least ten number-one hits—often taking over the first three spots on the Billboard charts. The TV specials are on nine networks and cassette/CD sales are in the gazillions!

Perhaps we've finally realized the truth: *God is much more concerned that we know him and love him and treat our neighbors well than he is with silly things like percussion instruments.*

A new shawl to wear over that

old black dress will put you in the

mood to *cel-e-bra-a-ate!* My new shawl

is pale gray and black cut velvet.

With long silky fringe. Very dramatic!

Now if someone would just

invite me to a party!

Chapter Two

There Are Parties, and Then There Are PARTIES!

Most people recognize the name Doug Oldham. He's the large man with the even larger voice you see on television occasionally and on some of the Homecoming tapes. Doug's voice introduced the Bill and Gloria Gaither music to the world some thirty years ago. "Thanks to Calvary, I Don't Live Here Anymore" was Doug's personal testimony. Who would think this sweet-spirited man who had sung for the Queen of England could have been a mean-spirited father and husband before allowing God to take control of his life? When Doug sang that song, he wept and his audiences wept. When he sang "A Rich Man Am I," people smiled. Often he *whistled* the first verse as he strolled down the aisle from the rear of the auditorium, touching, hugging, and shaking hands with those along the way. Doug was the first (long before Elvis!) to sing "He Touched Me."

Wayne and I met Doug and Laura Lee (and the Gaithers) in the early days of the Christian music business. Before the late sixties, gospel music wasn't much of a business at all, but rather a haphazard kind of *I'll sing in your church if you'll take up an offering to get me to the next town down the road.* Not unlike the *Smoke on the Mountain* Sanders family.

Oh, the hours spent defending the new sounds of gospel music! And oh, the hours spent celebrating it! Partying, if you will. A new release, a new artist, a newly crafted song, *or nothing at all* called for a get-together—sometimes on the Benson houseboat or at a restaurant (often we'd all pile onto someone's bus and head to Ashland City for catfish), but most of the time at one of our homes. Our husbands and their cohorts—songwriters, arrangers, conductors, pickers, grinners, and recording artists—seemed to be most able to conduct high business dealings in the midst of what could best be described as chaos. I have fond memories of Rick Powell (conductor, composer, arranger) sitting on the floor of my living room, calmly writing orchestra arrangements for the next day's sessions, yet not missing a beat when it came to playing with the kids and interacting in the animated conversation around him.

We wives rarely knew who would show up for dinner. Not just individual recording artists like Stuart Hamblin and Dave Boyer, but whole groups: Regeneration, Truth, the Oak Ridge Boys, the Imperials, and the Gaithers. We learned to cook in quantity. At the very last minute, after one of our husbands had called to warn us, Joy MacKenzie, Peggy Benson, Sylvia Powell, and I would burn up the phone lines with our, "You bring this; I'll bring that." Sometimes it was so very last minute that the orders were, "Bring whatever you have, and get here!" We thrived on those dynamics and didn't care a whit about impressing one another. We were ready to celebrate!

The best parties of all were given by the Oldhams. While the others of us tended, out of necessity, to throw our food together and slap it on paper plates, the Oldhams would plan ahead and put time and effort into the "doings" and "fixings" that made an invitation to their home a treasure.

Doug and Laura Lee lived in a one-hundred-year-old house in Franklin, just outside of Nashville. Going there was like visiting

Tara. Tall ionic pillars that went straight through the clouds all the way to heaven greeted you as you came up the driveway. When you stepped through the front door, you experienced another feast for the eyes: soaring ceilings with thick, ornate hand-carved moldings, and hardwood floors so shiny you could eat lunch on them. Skinny, tall windows so old and so prism-intense that when the sun hit just right, you couldn't help yourself—you had to take a step backward and simply admire! At night your eyes turned skyward, or at least *ceiling-ward*, where the relic, crystal chandeliers with their many-candled branches became a glorious refractory of light and color.

The furniture (Louie the something, I'm sure!)—wardrobes, buffets, and china cabinets of great enormity—had big, fat animal feet and exquisite lines that even a swan would covet. If you didn't know better you'd think the stuff was stolen from Buckingham Palace! Through the years, Doug and Laura had collected a wonderful assortment of hand-painted china and crystal that *sang* when you accidentally bumped it against the almost-too-precious-to-touch heavy English silver. The massive serving pieces were surely fit for a king! And us!

As we stepped into this world of a bygone era, the word "grandiose" never entered our minds. "Gracious" did! The Oldhams were at their happiest serving others. From the homemade, best-I've-ever-eaten varieties of soup to the lovingly prepared desserts, everything was perfect. Yet, what I remember most is that the atmosphere was as comfortable as grandma's feather bed.

Nothing lasts forever, though, and in time the Oldhams moved away from Nashville. At the present time they live in Virginia. Not long ago, I had the joyous opportunity to attend the wedding of Doug and Laura's youngest daughter, Dee. The ceremony was held at the end of a dirt road in a quaint, white-frame church—ancient cemetery on one side and pasture of grazing cows on the other. Huge trees tied with humongous pink bows were profuse in fall wardrobe. The bride wore the prettiest dress I've ever seen—white heavy satin with wide pink trim and dragging-to-the-floor bows. From the waist down, the groom was totally country—jeans and cowboy boots. From the waist up he was tuxedo uptown!

We all stayed in a wonderful place—a historic one-hundred-and-fifty-year-old inn—in Appomattox, with all the Oldham touches you would expect: flower-sweet rooms just meant for reminiscing, sugar-sweet iced-tea (the house wine of the South) served in crystal goblets along with good food, and the *oh-so-comfortably-sweet* atmosphere I remember from years gone by.

Equally precious, old memories and new! Cheap hamburger concoctions on paper plates after having spent the day juggling the schedules of our kids and husbands. Those precious moments of leisure time spent in front of a blazing fire, savoring the delectable offerings of Doug and Laura Lee. A wedding just last month. There are parties and *there are parties*, but sometimes they all run together and simply become one wonderful memory.

Soups from the Kitchen of Laura Lee Oldham

"Quick recipes," I said. "Women today need quick!" Laura Lee came through with the following. It would help if you owned a magnificent tureen or two as she does, but if not, just serve it out of the pan.

❧ Tomato Celery Soup from Shakertown, Kentucky

› Sauté together:

 1 small chopped onion

 ½ c. finely chopped celery

 2 t. butter

› Add:

 ⅛ t. pepper

 1 t. sugar

1 t. minced parsley
1 t. lemon juice
¼ t. salt
1 can tomato soup
1 can water
> Top with unsweetened whipped cream and parsley.

❤ Quick Broccoli Soup
> 1 or 2 packages frozen broccoli with cheese sauce (chop broccoli, or blend if you wish)
> Add 1 or 2 cans chicken broth
> Add a little real cream to taste.

❤ Laura Lee's Mushroom Soup
> Saute fresh sliced mushrooms, onions, and a fair amount of garlic in a deep pan with butter. Sprinkle granulated beef bouillon over it. When it is cooked a little, add half & half (the real stuff, not two percent!). Serve with crisp croutons.

❤ Quick Chowder (Laura tells me that this recipe came from Sharon Walker—a mutual friend—who is a pastor's wife in Michigan)
> 1 can Campbells corn chicken chowder
> 1 can chicken bouillon or broth
> 2 or 3 fat slices of Velvetta cheese to taste

All this soup talk reminded me that soup isn't soup without cornbread. Check out this **Broccoli Cornbread!**
> 2 boxes Jiffy Mix Cornbread
> 2 sticks butter or margarine, melted
> 4 eggs
> 10 oz. frozen broccoli (thawed)

- 8 oz. cottage cheese
- onion flakes
- Bake 25–45 minutes in a 9 x 13 inch pan at 350°

Chapter Three

Don't Turn Your Back on Gloria Gaither. I'm Warning You!

I n order to meet your expectations for this book, I'm including a certain amount of honest-to-goodness gossip. Some of you are expecting it. You're waiting with baited breath. Beads of perspiration are glistening on your brow. Even now, you're wringing your hands in anticipation. You whine in misery "Now! Now! Tell it to me now!"

Others of you are gathering your self-righteous skirts about you, looking askance at the page, making that dreadful tsk-tsk-ing sound with your tongue! "I will not listen to idle talk—I will not, I will not, I will not!" you say. I say, "Oh come on, give it a chance!"

First of all, let me say that in my humble opinion, gossip has taken a bad rap. It's such a negative in some circles that you have to disguise it as a prayer request. Don't look shocked, it happens all the time!

In the second place, not all gossip is *bad* gossip. There are three kinds: *nasty* gossip, *newsy* gossip, and *nosy* gossip. Think of it as the three Ns. Nasty gossip, of course, is bad. Newsy gossip is good; I thrive on it! And as to nosy, I try not to do it, but try as I might, I can't *not* do it (for instance, telling you what's in Sheila Walsh's closet), so I guess you could say I do it, but I'm not proud of it and often don't admit to it. If it's wrong, I'm asking God to forgive me here and now. Wait! That sounds just the slightest bit defensive, doesn't it?

Here are some little tidbits that fall into the category of *nosy* gossip. Gloria Gaither is one of my best friends (and my writing partner), and I would walk on my lips before I'd say anything *really bad* about her . . . BUT! I can tell you stuff! Like when I first met her, in those early days of the Benson company, first walked into her kitchen, I practically thrust my head into the sink and said, "Conditioner please." Her kitchen looked like a beauty shop! It had red velvet wallpaper! To tell the truth, flocked paper was *in* at the time, but nevertheless! Another time when I opened her refrigerator, I yelled bloody murder, thinking she had dead mice in her cheese bin. It was mold! Mold, mind you! Well, actually, my cheese bin wasn't much better, but that's beside the point.

Here is some *newsy* gossip about Gloria. She is not only a writer of great renown, a lyricist, a communicator, a scholar with degrees out the wazoo, but she is an authority on John Steinbeck (I barely know one piano from another!). She's even been approached to write a Broadway play based on his life and works.

There's more! Velvet walls aside, she is as good a decorator as you can find in Dallas, Atlanta, and Peoria all put together! But don't you dare turn your back on her; she's so decisive and fast she'll decorate the room right out from under you. Whether it's her home, her children's homes, her office, Bill's office, the Gaither Music Company offices, the studios, or the Homecoming video sets, her touch is magic. But no place showcases Gloria's talent more than Gaither Family Resources.

It's interesting how this state-of-the-future retail store came to be. For years, fans and friends alike nagged Bill and Gloria to create a place to showcase the mementos from their career. No one wanted to say the word *museum* right out loud, but that's exactly what they were thinking. "Perhaps Anderson College would be the place to put it," folks mused. After all that's where the Gaithers went to college. In their mind's eye, I'm sure the fans were picturing a room full of those hokey displays that showcase everything except a person's socks and underwear.

There would be Bill's very first upright piano with keys so old they made you think of bad teeth, ragged sheet music with curled edges, ancient concert tickets, and a plethora of pictures: with the kids, without the kids, Gloria on a bad hair day, Bill on a worse one!

A walk-through replica of the first touring bus would be a must! And the big, glass, padlocked cabinets encasing the performing outfits would be so popular there would

Praise the Lord, O my soul: all my inmost being, praise his holy name.
—Psalm 103:1

have to be one of those armed guards standing ominously to the side, guarding against unscrupulous polyester thieves.

After the museum idea was officially rejected, the idea for Gaither Family Resources took root in Gloria's mind and evolved into what it is today: a destination location for shopping, entertainment, personal growth, and fellowship. Not a moldy old museum, but a place of warmth and welcome that deserves its maxim: Real Resources for the Real Needs of Real People.

Nowhere are Gloria's decorating talents more evident than in the store, from the cozier-than- Cracker Barrel front porch, to the comfy wicker rocking chairs in front of the mega-sized video screen, to the coffee shop with homemade lattes and soups. But don't turn your back; she's forever redecorating. Always changing things!

I, for one—and I think Gloria would agree—believe that where and how you make your nest makes a measurable difference in how you view the world and how you live your life. It's not about having enough credit to buy a whole room full of furniture from a showroom; it's about collecting and accumulating things you love that make you content. So don't be afraid to gather around you—in your home, or your cubby at work—the treasures that cause you to celebrate the mundane, the ordinary day. Things that say *warmth and welcome*. Later in the book I'll give you specifics, a virtual *how-to* from Gloria Gaither. Something to look forward to!

Chapter Four

You Can Feel Pretty Shabby When You Go to a Slumber Party with Vestal

If anyone has a party heart, it's Vestal Goodman. I knew it when I met her thirty years ago, and it's true today. This next item falls into the *nosy-newsy* gossip category. Listen closely, lean closer! *Vestal Goodman's pajamas are even more festive than the clothes she wears on stage!* It's no wonder Howard is out of breath!

One night not long ago in Gatlinburg, Vestal showed up in Gloria's room, where we'd promised to meet for an after-concert girlfriend thing, dolled-up in this red and black satin oriental number that made us think we'd entered the presence of a Chinese empress. Her hair had been spiffied; her make-up had been spiffied; her nails were perfect; *she was perfect!* Right down to her little black velvet slippers, she was perfect! The rest of us were in faded sweats and flannel uglies; nothing about us had been spiffied since the break of dawn!

I love being friends with Vestal, although truthfully, when you first meet her, long before you see her in her pj's, you can feel quite intimidated by her. It's not just the flamboyant clothes, it's that *wherever, whenever,* she's so . . . so . . . the center of attention! She doesn't try to be, *she just is!*

I think of her as a cross between the effusive star of Broadway, Ethel Merman, and the dynamic luminary of opera, Maria Callas.

Like Merman, Vestal is a bigger-than-life persona and has the most unique of voices. An instrument she can bend around a musical phrase, and then in her *belt-it-out* delivery, fling it through the airwaves to it's destination: smack-dab in your face, in your psyche, and in your soul.

I've been awed, when watching a crowd of twenty thousand in a sold-out arena, as people worship, praise, and celebrate in glorious response to Vestal and the Goodmans. I've been even more blown away, in the intimate setting of the famed House of Blues (in New Orleans, during a Christian Booksellers showcase) at the excitement Vestal can create with the hip young people who, that day, screamed and applauded in raucous ovation. It's amazing, the cross-generational appeal of this spirited woman.

Vestal could have been another Callas. She started out to train as an opera singer. She had the refined voice for it, but to make a long story short, she was swept off her feet by Howard who was holding tent revivals all over the south, married him, and became his solo act. One day when a tornado came through, ripped down the tent, and took the public address system to the next county, she found herself standing in a field before an audience with nothing but her voice. She was madder than a wet hen that Howard had put her in such a predicament, but nevertheless she opened her mouth and sang. She would deal with Howard later! Lo and behold, out came not the refined voice of an opera diva, but the powerful gospel sound that's been wowing audiences ever since!

Like Callas, Vestal understands *presence,* that you must present yourself well in the big picture of performance. Somehow I doubt Maria bathed her performances in prayer, as I know Vestal to do, but she certainly knew there was more to it than opening your mouth and lettin' it fly. Callas was known to be nearly *possessed* by her passion of this "big picture concept," and tried to teach it to others. Case in point was when she said to a student: ". . . and for heaven's sake, get a look." She was trying to get across a mandate that can now be found in each and every how-to manual for wanna-be's. *If you want to be a star, then look like a star.* People expect it!

Vestal Goodman has a look, and a presence! Once you've watched her perform, you'll never forget her. She wears the most flamboy-ant clothes. I like that in a person. Rumor has it she is imitated in big city drag clubs right along with Streisand, Channing, and Cher. If that information causes you to stumble, please calm down and think! To perform as Vestal, you would have to study her, learn her songs, and duh! *Vestal sings the gospel!*

When she is approached by one of these characters (and yes, they have been known to show up at Homecoming concerts), Vestal opens her arms in warm embrace and (as she does with most anyone) says, "I love you, darlin'." Given the chance, there will be a layin' on of hands and a prayer meeting. Praying, not that a person will renounce a lifestyle, but simply that he or she will know Jesus.

Vestal is a good example of a celebratory heart. Her group isn't called the Happy Goodmans for nothin'! And she is a great exam-ple of a person who has been surprised by God. He has used her to reach thousands in ways she couldn't have imagined. Really, who else do you know with a ministry to cross-dressers?

God may have a surprise or two for you. For me! Get ready! But for heaven's sake, do I have to tell you? *Get a look!*

Chapter Five

It's Never Too Late to Be a Nerd. A Word-Nerd That Is!

Each day when I turn on my computer and check my e-mail, I find a "word of the day" from Tanya Goodman Sykes. Tanya's claim to fame is that she is a niece of Vestal (daughter of Rusty Goodman who is Howard's deceased brother), wife of Michael Sykes of Ponder, Sykes and Wright, and a talented vocalist and lyricist in her own right. I'm one of many friends on her list. With the word comes its meaning, the proper pronunciation, and a sentence of Tanya's own making that uses the word correctly and is relevant to whatever is going on in the world. For instance, the day after the presidential inauguration her word was *denouement* (day noo MA), meaning, "a final part in which everything is made clear and no questions or surprises remain." Her sentence was, "It was gratifying to finally reach the denouement of the presidential election on Saturday."

When I asked her how she came to this interest in words, Tanya told me she couldn't remember when she wasn't intrigued by them. When she was six years old she would read anything; if there were no books, she'd read the back of a soap wrapper! In high school, she admits she wasn't the best of students, not because she wasn't intelligent, but because she just didn't put forth the effort. The exception was English, especially the reading assignments.

"That's where I excelled," she says proudly. "I was somewhat of a scholar." Tanya then takes me down a wonderful memory trail to introduce me to Mary Hart Finley, her honors English teacher at North Hopkins High School in Madisonville, Kentucky.

"Older than God, meaner than a snake, and as unkempt as a street person!" Tanya laughs. "She talked constantly about the p-sats and the nim-squats (The Preliminary Scholastic Aptitude Tests and the National Merit Scholarship Quality Tests), and you can imagine what we did with *that!* It was almost like she was *inviting* us to poke fun at her. P-sats and nim-squats!" After all these years Tanya can still laugh till tears roll down her cheeks at the memory.

"Oh, how that woman loved words!" Tanya reflects. "She had an incredible vocabulary, and she taught me to love words too! But never in a million years would I let that poor woman know. I didn't want her to have the satisfaction of knowing how much I loved that class. From the daily assignments to the quizzing and cramming for tests, I loved it all!" It's quiet for a moment, obviously Tanya has slipped into a time warp . . . back to North Hopkins High!

"Like here's a word I remember!" She practically jolts me out of my seat.

"Jerkin! Then you had multiple choice options."

"Small pickle," I say assuredly. "I know that one."

"Wrong!" she fairly shouts. "Nnnaaaa!" She makes that horrible nasal sound that imitates the buzzer on a TV game show when a wrong answer is given.

"*Small pickle!*" You would think the way Tanya is laughing that *small pickle* is the punch line to a joke.

"That was one of the choices. *Different spelling! Different word!* J-E-R-K-I-N." She is pronouncing each letter like I'm a third grader.

"It means jacket!" Do I detect a bit of self-righteousness in her voice?

"Jacket!" she repeats like I might have missed it the first ten times.

Gee! Somehow I feel as though I've been thoroughly corrected by old Mary Hart Finley herself and sent off to sit in the corner with a dunce cap on my head! No lunch; no recess! I *am* remembering vaguely that the pickle word starts with a *g* and has an *h* hidden somewhere within. Whatever! Never argue with old Mary-Hart-Goodman-Sykes!

"Let's face it, I'm a *word nerd!*" says Tanya, shaking off her high school teacher persona. "Everyone seems to like this e-mail thing; I get a lot of comments back."

If the truth be known, I can relate to Tanya. She was self-admittedly a lousy student, and I wasn't much better. You wouldn't exactly say I was *lousy,* I was just *disinterested.* I had other fish to fry. What amazes us both—and we've had discussions before—is that in spite of the fact that we were less than prepared for life educationally, God figured out what to do with us!

Perhaps it takes God a little longer to figure out where some people fit, and he has to think about it for awhile. In some cases, he lets us fall in the mud and wallow awhile to learn some valuable lessons. Maybe he came to the conclusion that if nothing else, Tanya and I would be an encouragement to others, to women who feel as though they've wasted all their opportunities and that life has passed them by. *If Sue can speak and write books—in light of the fact she goofed away her college years hav-*

> *Praise the Lord, O my soul, and forget not all his benefits!*
> —Psalm 103:2

ing a good time—anyone can find something to be successful at. If Tanya—considering she was rotten to the core, making a total fool of you-know-who—can write those incredible songs, and sing them as she does with the voice of an angel, then there is hope for me.

You may not think so at the moment, dear reader, but there is hope! I meet women week in and week out for whom it wasn't too late. At thirty! At forty! At fifty! At seventy-five! New ideas! New energy! New careers! New opportunities! And here's a little secret: More times than not, the joy runs deeper and the rewards seem greater when you've gotten there the hard way . . . or the stupid way!

You've just found out your husband got a promotion, or your child made the team, or you feel like celebrating on a moment's notice for no earthly reason. Pick up fast food, pull out a pretty table cloth and the good china, stuff fresh flowers in a vase, turn on some music, light a few candles, and go for it! In that setting even corn dogs taste good.

Celebrating the Everyday-ness of Life!

Anyone can gear up for the big stuff—birthdays, Christmas, Thanksgiving, even Ground Hog Day—but it takes a little effort to celebrate the ordinary, the mundane, the humdrum. Let's face it, it's downright hard! First of all, life isn't what we thought it would be. We married for money and found out our husbands only made minimum wage. We go to a bank that offers "no points loans" and they look at us and say "there's no point." We slave all day over a take-out menu and nobody thanks us!

You've heard the jokes! You've also heard the platitudes: "Turn your lemons into lemonade." "Smile and the world smiles with you." Blah, blah, blah . . . whatever! In this section of the book you'll find help! You'll learn that having an advisory board is a must, and time management is a possibility. You can have permission to clean out your closet; using Sheila Walsh as your example—this is the moment you've all been waiting for, *information worth the price of the book*—throw out the drab and keep only the colorful.

Speaking of colorful, if you put only a few of Gloria Gaither's suggestions for using color to create a more joyous home into practice,

I can tell you unequivocally, it will improve your mood.. And please, dear reader, don't think I'm judging! It's just that I've known people who have been in a bad mood for so long they don't remember what a good mood feels like. If you are one of those people, heaven forbid, only you can change it.

And have you ever taken a drive on a fall day and looked out the window? No! I mean *really looked out the window?* Soaked in the beauty of God's colorful artwork? If you go with me on a little trek through the countryside, it will put a party in your heart and on your face too! I'll even give you the recipe for my mama's pumpkin pie!

All of these external things are useful and undoubtedly will help you create a whole new paradigm for yourself—one of turning *ho-hum* into *celebration!* You'll love hearing the inside scoop of how my crazy friends do it. But here is the clincher, and probably the most important truth in this book: If your *true identity* isn't based on being a child of God and understanding that as his heir you have unlimited perks, you may as well give up now. Your identity, your worth, can only come from knowing who you are in Christ.

Liz Curtis Higgs has been God's catalyst to help me better understand the concept, and she'll help you too. Read on!

Chapter Six

I Don't Really Care If I Lose My Shirt (I Have More), but I'd Sure Hate to Lose My Mind and My Friends!

In the book *Ten Tips for Women Who Want to Change the World Without Losing their Friends, Shirts, or Minds,* the author suggests you assemble a committee of mentors you can call on for advice. She says you don't have to know them; they can actually be in your imagination. This is probably not unlike what Hillary *really* meant when she talked about communicating with Eleanor Roosevelt. Now, dear reader, please don't take that to mean *I'm best friends with Mrs. Clinton;* we've never even met. We could never be shopping buddies, I promise you; but be honest, do you really think she was having séances? Puh-leeze!

My mother died eighteen years ago, and I talk to her all the time. Okay, I know your hair is standing on end, so I'll be quick to say that *the conversation is totally one-sided!*

"Sorry Mama, I know better!" I say toward heaven as I put a milk carton on the table—something she never would have done.

"Don't look!" I say as I line a pie tin with a store-bought crust, or dust the kitchen floor with my sock foot and slide the crumbs under the rug.

The point is, my mother is still my mentor, my advisor. "What would Mother do in this situation?" I often ask myself.

While I'd never even thought about having a board of directors before, I'm warming to the idea. It sounds so official!

"This is a decision for my board," you could say, which is far better than saying, "I'll check with my dead mother." In Christian circles, you would be history, even though all you'd be doing is trying to figure out what your mother would do, given the circumstances.

You could even blame your advisors when you don't want to do something. "Sorry! I ran it by my board and they vetoed it!"

Another of my so-called board members who has also moved to the great beyond, would be Miss Florence Stephenson, a tall, stately member of our church when I was a child. She wore her hair piled high and on Sunday mornings wore fabulous hats and gloves. Sometimes there was an animal that bit its own tail flung around her neck. All this adornment made her stand out in a sea of drabness. She was my Sunday school teacher and taught me Scripture and its importance in everyday life. Those verses have sustained me, comforted me, and empowered me at every turn of the road. Not only in dealing with cancer, but in facing so many of life's overwhelming interferences. (For those of you who have heard me speak, it is Miss Stephenson on whom my Mrs. Vandertweezers character is based.)

All of my mentors aren't dead. Some you've met in this book. One is my cousin Nancy, who lives on a farm in Ohio. Our mothers were cousins, but they were as close as sisters. Nancy and I talk often, and I draw wisdom and soul-sustaining nourishment from her.

"Oh, my darling," she says. "God is so trustworthy. He is so good. We must take it a day at a time, and he will never leave us or forsake us. He promised! You can count on it!" Sometimes board members just have to remind you of the basics.

I like this idea of having an advisory board. Think about it! A board of godly women (alive and dead) that you don't even have to talk to. Just thinking about them causes you to want to do what is right! And if it's true that having such mentors will help me change the world without losing friends, shirt, or mind (sort of a variation on the Great Commission), all the better! Only one problem! As to losing my mind, it might be a little too late.

Having a party? Having guests over? Prepare for it in your mind long before you clean the house and cook the food. Picture everyone having a good time, smiling and engaged in good conversation. See yourself relaxed and enjoying your friends, as opposed to fretting over the details.

Chapter Seven

A Perfect House Is the Sign of a Boring Woman, but That Doesn't Mean You Can't Manage Your Time Better

*C*huck and Marsha Blackburn are in my Sunday night church fellowship group. Marsha is a Tennessee state senator and the group's connection to politics. We rely on her to help us understand issues, both on national and local levels, and we're hoping that someday she'll become governor, but for our own very self-serving reason: We think it would be so cool to have "group" in the governor's mansion every Sunday night!

One of Marsha's strengths is that she's a time-management expert. I asked her to give me a few tips for this book. After all, how can you have a party goin' on in your heart (or home) if you are totally bogged down with all the details of life? Marsha's suggestions will help you. My comments are in parentheses and probably won't be much help at all.

Ways to Get More Than Twenty-Four Hours out of Each Day

Courtesies
🖤 Thank you notes—hand-written notes—are a must for

kindnesses received. Make this task easy by simply address-
ing the envelope, inserting the card, and putting it in your
day book (or as in my case, shopping bag). Then when you
have a spare moment—stopped still in traffic, the doctor's
office, waiting for a child at dance lessons—write your note
and drop it off at a post office box.

🖤 Stock a gift drawer (in my case, the top of a closet) where you
can quickly "shop" for a gift. This is a terrific way to insure
that you never show up at a friend's home, or hospital bed,
emptyhanded.

🖤 For handcrafted gifts, keep a piece of needlepoint or cross
stitch in the glove box of the car. It's a great stress reliever,
easy to pick up during ball games and idle moments, and a
perfect personalized gift item for close friends. (Make no mistake, I've done a few needlepoint pillows in my lifetime, and I've
knitted shawls, sweaters, skirts, and one whole suit. Let's just say
those days are over, due to lack of interest.)

🖤 RSVP both to save embarrassment and out of courtesy. (If you
didn't listen when your mama taught you this, you should be
ashamed of yourself!)

🖤 At the beginning of the year, update your day book with birthday information. Be sure to send birthday cards to friends and
loved ones. Then remember to transfer to the next year's cal-
endar. (Couldn't agree more!)

🖤 Stay in contact with old friends. One note or card each week
is a great goal. Just think, that's fifty-two special "hellos" each
year. (My new goal!)

Organization

🖤 Pack your car at night with everything you need for the next
day's activity and work. (I've done this, and it makes me drive
down the road purrin' like a kitten.)

❤ Prioritize your work, duties, and responsibilities. Handle the high-priority items first. If you prioritize, you will find that some items will actually *fall off* your to-do list. (*I do this every day of my life, but please don't tell my friends and spoil my image.*)

❤ Organize your to-do list by divisions: family, personal, work, charity.

❤ Keep a note pad in your car, by the bed, and at the kitchen sink. When a thought pops into your head, write it down. (*This works! As a writer, I live by it.*)

❤ Make plans for your life. Set goals for each day, week, and certainly for the year. (*I highly recommend!*)

❤ Call ahead to confirm appointments. (*Or speaking dates.*)

❤ Get directions before you leave for a destination. (*Oh my! Should we tell our husbands this?*)

❤ Return phone calls while you do the laundry. (*Or other mindless tasks.*)

❤ Plan to have fun. Schedule lunch with friends, dinners out, parties together. Make a few minutes for daily email, notes, and messages on voice mail.

❤ Live by a budget. (*Whoops!*)

❤ Don't lose your belongings. If you loan it out, write it down. (*With the exception of two things: umbrellas and Tupperware. Umbrellas should be public property. You should be able to put one down when you are finished with it, pick one up when you need one. Tupperware should be continually circling the globe, being filled and refilled, being the blessing God intended it to be.*)

❤ Double-team your menial tasks. When you are waiting on something or someone, have another simple task you can be completing. (*Dana has a picture of me in a dressy white suit and high heels, sitting on the floor in the bathroom, cleaning out under the sink. I do this one well!*)

❤ Turn off the TV. Watching mindless TV programs just uses up time that can never be replaced. (*Duh! We must get this through our Clairol heads!*)

Household

♥ Organize your house cleaning so you take on one major project each week—wash cabinets, clean doors, clean out drawers. (*Have you ever seen the cartoon with the woman and the cat with the caption: "What the woman says: 'Oh, sweet baby, I love you so much . . .,' and "What the cat hears: 'Blah, blah, blah, blah, blah . . .'"? My answer to this one is, "Blah, blah, blah! I can't hear you!"*)

♥ Build a wall of pantry shelves in your garage or utility room. Stock your bulk purchase items in this area. Keep it inventoried so that you know what you have and what you need. (*Mine is in the utility room.*)

♥ Set aside one evening each season to clean closets, toss what you don't need, and make a shopping list of needed items. Do this with each member of your family. (*Blah, blah, blah, again!*)

♥ Decide on a basic color scheme, have a style of furniture for your house, and stick with it. This way, you can shop as you go. It also makes giving gifts to you easier in that people will pretty much know what you like. (*Eeeek! Is "gypsy" a style? I'm a very easy person to buy gifts for! Anything goes!*)

♥ Water your house plants by placing them outside on a rainy day. (*Sometimes.*)

♥ Don't try to be a perfectionist. If the task really isn't that important, perform to get it successfully completed. Let "good enough" be good enough! (*This is the best suggestion yet! Joy MacKenzie has a sign in her entryway that says, "Show Me a Perfect House, and I'll Show You a Boring Woman." I couldn't agree more. The only perfectionist I want to know is a plastic surgeon!*)

♥ Tackle your major renovation and cleaning chores one at a

time. Focus on one project, see it through to completion, and then turn your attention to another.

Clothes

- ❦ Have your children lay out their clothes for the next day. You do the same thing.

- ❦ Keep a 3x5 card in your wallet or a list in your Day Timer. List clothing items that are needed by you and your family members. This makes it easier to sale shop and take advantage of bargains. (*Marsha is the ultimate sale shopper. She's also our best-dressed, most clothes-knowledgeable group member. I call her when I need wardrobe help. In fact, she is the one who taught me to buy a dozen pair of pantyhose at a time so I wouldn't have to think of it again for awhile. She's worth the big bucks I pay her [not] just for advice like that.*)

- ❦ Let your fingers do the walking across the Internet. To save time and travel, do your information gathering and shopping over the Internet when possible.

- ❦ Shop the sales racks first.

- ❦ Flip through fashion magazines before you even touch a rack.

- ❦ Keep a sewing kit handy. Scissors, needle, thread for quick hems, stitch witchery, and double-faced hemming tape. (*Eeeek again! I have a shopping bag where I stash my mending. When the bag is full, I drop it off down the street at Laura's house. She is in charge of my mending and alterations. It makes me a nicer person.*)

- ❦ Buy a good clothing steamer. (*Marsha has nagged me about this forever. Okay, okay! I'm headed to Wal-Mart!*)

- ❦ Buy clothing items and seasonal supplies at the end of the season. (*Or at the beginning, or the middle, or the end!*)

- ❦ Build your wardrobe along a color scheme. (*Since I have a ministry to the gaudy, I wouldn't touch that one on a bet!*) Use basic colors, then choose accessories with the new hot shades and styles. Don't be dull, but don't build on fads. Take time to keep up on trends.

☙ Keep a shoe care kit next to the spot where you keep your shoes. Clean up when you take your shoes off. (*Does handing them to your husband count?*)

Groceries and Household Supplies

☙ Head to the grocery store with a list. Go at odd hours and never on the weekend except in an emergency. (*Did I ever tell you about the night Wayne and I set the alarm for three* A.M. *just to find out who in the world shops at Wal-Mart in the middle of the night?*)

☙ When you finish dinner at night, do pre-prep for the next night's meal. (*Wayne and I plan ahead by cooking large quantities that we can eat as leftovers. Soup, a pork roast with turnips and parsnips, chicken and rice, or a pasta dish.*)

☙ Buy anything you use regularly in bulk quantities at the wholesaler or warehouse store. This saves shopping time and money. (*This doesn't work for me, except for paper and cleaning products. When I buy food in bulk, it often goes to waste.*)

☙ Keep your grocery list going. Make it a work in progress. When you get close to the bottom of the jar, add it to the list so that you purchase a replacement before it means a special trip to the store. (*I'm religious about this! It's good to be religious!*)

☙ Place small servings of leftovers in Zip Lock bags, label, and stick in the freezer. They make perfect quick and easy meals. (*I never label mine. It's part of the adventure! Sometimes I dump whatever is in the freezer into a pot of soup. It works!*)

☙ Keep a box of baking soda open in the back of the refrigerator to keep it odor-free. (*Well, duh, Marsha! Everyone knows that!*)

At the Office

☙ When chairing a meeting, have a written agenda and distribute it in advance. (*As the former vice-president of a company, I can agree. Many times, even though I was the least important person there, my agenda became gospel simply because I was the only one who had one.*)

♥ Make notes on the back of business cards that you pick up along the way. Note the who, what, when, and where. (*I must begin to do this! I'm sick of being confused over business cards.*)

♥ Don't open your mouth unless you have something worthwhile to say. If you will do this, you will find you don't have to go back and apologize for speaking out of school. (*Guilty!*)

♥ Organize your work area. Keep the items you use most often closest to you. (*Like chocolate!*)

♥ Work on your toughest assignments when your energy level is the highest. (*Yes!*)

♥ Use technology to get yourself organized. Caller ID, email, voice mail, fax machine will all add minutes to the day.

♥ When you need to work uninterrupted, place a "Do Not Disturb" sign in view of anyone who may distract you. (*Personally, I'm in favor of distractions.*)

♥ As you accept a new project, make a new file. Keep everything associated with that project—phone slips, email copies, research, and so forth—in that file. (*This is my worst problem, not being able to organize. Sometimes I spend a half-day organizing and still end up with one big stack labeled "miscellaneous."*)

Chapter Eight

If This Was Rotary Club, Sheila and Barry Would Be Voted Out!

Sheila Walsh, her husband Barry Pfaeler, and their son Christian, are members of our fellowship group too. "Officially" they belong, but they rarely come because they are always on the road. Sheila speaks to an average of fifteen thousand women every weekend, and not only does Women of Faith keep them busy, but they have many other career demands. I don't want to seem ruthless, but if this was Rotary, they would have been kicked out by now.

It's actually a privilege to be part of a group such as ours, so truthfully, I'm sure they would be there if they could. If nothing else, a person would come to our group for the food. When our church set up the guidelines (thank heaven they weren't rules) for fellowship groups, they suggested that we not do food, only popcorn and drinks. It was thought that bringing food might become a responsibility and thus a hindrance to some. They didn't know our bunch!

We take that Bible verse seriously that says, "Where two or three are gathered, one brings baked beans, another chips and dip, and another chocolate cream pie with meringue piled up to heaven!"

Our tables look like Thanksgiving every Sunday night. Everyone likes to cook, including most of the men; and even if it's left-overs, they're of the gourmet variety. Perhaps Thanksgiving isn't an accurate comparison, since we never check with each other; it's totally uncoordinated. It could better be called "Thanksglomeration," and we like it that way.

We all love to be heard (sometimes loudly!), so there are always discussions going on. Sometimes as a group, sometimes in small huddles. I'm happy to say we've solved most of the problems of the world, the church, and each other! But the most important and meaningful thing we do each week before the evening is over is go around the circle and talk about what's going on in our lives, then pray each request, need, or expression of thanksgiving.

We sometimes say, "If those Pfaelers don't come to group, we're just going to stop praying for them. That'll fix 'em!" We won't of course, but we may give them demerits!

During the Christmas season this year, when Barry and Sheila had a few weeks off, I assumed we would be invited to have group at their house. If nothing else, I thought, we could make them feel guilty, *pressure* them, if you will, into inviting us. In light of their delinquencies, it's the least they could do. With that in mind, I thought of you, dear reader, and realized how fun it would be to peek into Sheila's closet and report back. I could tell you if it's neat or messy, how many pairs of shoes she has, and how it breaks down. Like say, out of ten pairs, three might be sporty, two sandals, three pumps, and two pairs of boots. And if perchance her closet is *overflowing* with shoes, I could approximate the number and do an analysis comparing her quantity to some other in-the-limelight figure like . . . who? Imelda Marcos maybe?

The problem is, they didn't invite us. Her mother was visiting and sick; Christian was sick; the dog was sick. Blah, blah, blah, excuses, excuses! By this time, however, I'm getting very impatient.

I'm determined to look in that closet. *I'm obsessed!* But how? I thought about those old episodes of "I Love Lucy" and how she disguised herself as a plumber or painter or prospective maid.

I put on a painter's outfit, complete with mustache, and tried to remember how to paint. Do the brush strokes go vertical or horizontal? And what do you do when you come to a doorknob? Then it occurred to me! *They wouldn't let me in if they hadn't ordered a painter.*

As to masquerading as a maid, the fingernails would give me away. And is it Lysol you use on the floors? Or is it Pledge? Trying a break-in was out of the question too. They live in a gated community called Fort Knox. Well, not really Fort Knox, but you get the picture.

A week or two after Christmas I called Barry and casually suggested that I drop by to give them their Christmas gifts. (An eight-dollar box of Frango mints and a twelve-dollar toy for Christian from Pier 1, if you must know. It's the thought that counts, and the thought in this case was, *I gotta see in that closet!)*

"Please come! Any time!" Barry said enthusiastically. Why hadn't I thought of this approach sooner? Duh!

They greeted me warmly, apologized for the mess (they'd just moved from three doors up the street for reasons I won't go into), and we sat down at the kitchen table. Sheila plopped their gorgeous rag-doll cat in my lap, knowing how I love cats, and with my free hand I petted their cute little dog. They entertained me with delightful stories about Christian, who was taking a nap.

All I could think of was, *I gotta see in that closet.* Then, right out of the blue, Barry asked if I'd like to look around the new house. Do bears live in the woods? Does the Pope wear a beanie? Is this a window of opportunity if I ever saw one?

Well girlfriend! To make a long story short, even though it's too late for that, I soon found myself smack-dab in the middle of

Sheila's closet. A nice big closet, with Barry's duds on one side and Sheila's on the other.

"You won't believe it, but I just organized it myself this afternoon," Barry bragged. I believed! It was perfect, neat as a pin, not a belt or a tie out of place.

My eyes did a quick sweep and landed on a shelf high above our heads, on Barry's side, where two pairs of well-worn tennis shoes sat side by side.

"Those belonged to my mom and dad . . ." said Barry quietly, and I remembered that he'd lost both in recent months. ". . . just couldn't part with them. There's something about a person's everyday shoes that's so personal." I agreed. I was touched deeply, remembering that I still had my mother's lipstick, at least fifty tubes of it (she's been gone seventeen years), thinking they were just too personal to part with.

If I had to come up with one word that describes Sheila's closet, it would be "color." And knowing she is cutting edge when it comes to looking good, I was thinking, *This is a sign from God! A sign that we're done with those grays and tans, and oatmeal drabs; we're back to glorious color! Like Mama wore in the fifties! Greens, pinks, yellows, blues, and reds of every shade. And prints, stripes, and polka dots!* Wow! If Sheila is right, and Gloria is right about how color affects how we feel (read on), then we're all in for a major mood change. I'm ready!

Oh yes, one other thing I almost forgot. The answer to "how many pairs of shoes?" Perhaps a few more than Imelda!

Chapter Nine

Tips from Gloria for Creating a Home That Says Warmth and Welcome

Not long ago, I asked Gloria to give me some pointers for creating a home that exudes warmth and welcome so I could pass these valuable tips along to you, dear reader. We were spending Thanksgiving with Bill and Gloria at the time, so I had the opportunity to observe firsthand that Gloria does, in fact, practice what she preaches. I can vouch for the fact that she's passionate about the subject; we talked about it off and on all weekend. I made notes till my fingers were numb, so I would get it just right. No one says it quite like Gloria.

This much I knew beforehand, having been friends with Gloria for over thirty years: She believes that all spaces we human beings live in—homes, rooms, huts, cottages, cabins, barns—can be beautiful! I've heard her say it more than once: "A motel room, a hospital room, a dressing room, or any other borrowed place can be transformed by a lover of beauty and people." I've also heard her say that it's an ugly world we live in and that the soul craves, and must have, beauty. I agree!

As we were putting the house back together the day after Thanksgiving, she reminded me once again: "Beauty is the sweetest gift we can give those who share and visit our space." I've seen Gloria live this out. The "spaces" she inhabits are beautiful, sometimes just because she's moved things around and added a touch here and there, as evidenced with her store. The only time I've seen her fail is when we are sharing a hotel room when on a speaking tour. Heaven knows she's tried to make it beautiful, but it's hopeless because I'm so messy. (I like neatness at home, but in a hotel room, anything goes!) I think it's good that I bring out the messy in her; it gives her a chance to get it out of her system. Together, we throw wet towels around, drip makeup here and there, and hang our underwear on lamp shades. I've seen her really get into it! On the other hand, in a hotel room with Bill, she lights candles and plays soft music. (Heaven knows what she wears then, but I doubt it's the long-sleeved, shapeless, flannel gowns she wears when she rooms with me!)

Gloria gives God the credit for being the Originator and Provider of all that is beautiful. "Borrow and learn from nature," she tells me as we're deciding which of the leftovers to save. "To make a place at peace, bring nature inside. Shells, twigs, stones, leaves, flowers, buds, seeds, nuts, fruits, vegetables, and all living things—birds, insects, butterflies, creatures, great and small—can be used in decorating." I look around her big roomy kitchen with the fireplace and realize that's exactly what she's done. The evidence is everywhere, from the husks with dried corn on the mantle, to the big copper tub of gourds under the stairway, to strategically placed wooden bowls abundant with fruit. "Copy how nature arranges things, colors things, combines things. Use nature's sense of humor, whimsy, and surprise." Gloria moves around the room replenishing fruit bowls and nut jars.

"Even when making a silk flower arrangement, remember nothing in nature is straight and stiff." She stops, throws her hands in the air, and stiffens for a visual image of how nature is *not*. "Stems and blossoms are *wooed*,"—her word, not mine—"by the sun and will bend around any obstruction—even themselves—to get to the sun. Fan out silk leaves with your thumb; turn buds and blossoms toward the sky—no two exactly at the same angle; make stems crooked and vining." Again she uses her whole body to twist and turn, in imitation of nature's serendipitous behavior. I haven't seen silk arrangements in Gloria's house, but I make a note to check mine when I get home. My silk flowers could be dead by now for all I know, and I can promise you they haven't been *wooed*.

Now this next bit of wisdom is really profound, and as you can imagine, I wish I could take credit for it—it's so simple! "Use *generously* the colors nature uses *generously*. Use for accent, for drama, surprise, and interest the same colors nature uses for surprise or drama." I think of my own house and wonder if perhaps I've overdone it with the surprises. Gloria's observations make me realize my colors aren't always what you would call *natural*. Unless you call fluorescents natural. I comfort myself with the fact that people *do* seem to be surprised! (*But is that good?*" I ask myself.)

Gloria continues: "Start with lots of soothing,"—*soothing* did she say?—"greens, sky grays, and blues; sand and soil shades; wheat, barley, oat yellows, and neutrals. Especially for walls and floors, and coverings for big pieces of furniture. Then experiment with splashes of hot cornflower blue, poinsettia red, sunflower yellow, sunset magenta, foxglove purple, spring weeping willow chartreuse!" (If the songwriting thing doesn't work out she can get a job in a paint company naming the paints!) By now we're spiffying Bill and Gloria's bedroom, and it's all making sense. I've been in this room many times before, and yes, I'm sure I've said to myself, "This is a soothing place to be." I just never thought about it being planned!

"Choose colors for rooms according to what mood you most

desire to be exhibited in that room. Colors *do* affect behavior!"
Gloria continues assuredly. (Our bedroom has Renoir red carpet-
ing with lots of bright yellow and green . . . and oh yes, a little pink
and blue . . . and purp—oh, never mind!)

"A soft butter yellow tends to make one feel happy. We don't say
she has a sunny disposition for nothing!" (I'm shaking my head with
gusto. I love all shades of yellow!) This next I could have done
without: "Bullfighters use a red flag for a purpose, too. A red room
tends to agitate and make one explosive or passionate." (It's not
like Gloria hasn't seen my bedroom! I'm suddenly taking this personally! What could she be think-
ing? But she's on a roll! She's folding
towels like a maid at the Waldorf
who's being paid by the item. She
doesn't seem to know that the
rock from her sling-shot has burst
my pretty balloon.)

*G*uests are coming
and you haven't dusted
the house since
Christmas of 1998.
No problem. Light the
house with candles.

"Blue skies, smilin' at me . . ."
she sings enthusiastically. "Yes! It's
true! Light blue tends to make us
feel at peace, serene, settled and
relaxed." (I'm feeling slightly agi-
tated, unsettled! I'm still seeing
red!) "Not a good color for a work
area," she warns, "but a great color for a bedroom, bath, or sitting
room." (I can't seem to remember a single thing in my house that's
light blue—or light *anything* for that matter!)

"Greens tend to cool." (*At last!* I have greens in my family room.)
"A good color for rooms on the hot side of the house,"—let's see now,
which side is which?—"or a place where we exercise or work. It's a
cool-down color." (Wait! If it's in a room with a fireplace, does that
negate the premise?) "God used lots of green in the hot summer."

(We rarely go into that room in the summer. In fact, we call it our Christmas-tree room. Wrong again!)

By now Gloria and I are sitting in her den. Candles are lit all over the room. Music is playing. "The senses are an avenue to the soul," she says. (I'm agreeing, and my soul is so comfortable I might just take a nap. I've left my pad of paper somewhere—don't know, don't care—and I'm scrawling along the margins in a magazine.) "Think of the mind and soul as the center city, and the senses being interstates coming into the city from all directions. The more of these roads that are open, the more chance you have of visiting the city." (I'm a visual person, so I *get it;* even in my close-to-catatonic state, I get it.)

"Decorating should involve all of the senses. In every room there should be things that engage each of those senses: sight, smell, touch, sound, taste." (Yes, I agree completely! Everything about me feels engaged. Or disengaged. Whatever! My feet are on the footstool, and I'm slumping further and further into this comfortable no-man's-land nirvana. I nod both in drowsiness and in agreement.)

"There should be lovely things to *see,* like colors, art, fabrics, woods. Great *smells,* like coffee perking,"—it is!—"fragrant flowers, small pillows of spices on the bed, vanilla candles, a bundle of cinnamon sticks tied with ribbon." (There are!) "There should be *textures* and things to hold in one's hand—a smooth stone on an antique book,"—there is!—"fine wood grains,"—there are!— "smooth glass shelves or sculpture, fabrics of tweed, silk, velvet, corduroy, sheep's wool, marble, tiles, sculpture or plush carpet, braided rugs." (There is no braided rug that I can see from where I'm slouched, and I couldn't move if I had to; I'm getting the picture, and I couldn't agree more; I'm a texture person!)

"Sounds, there should be sounds!" she says forcefully and with great enthusiasm. I jump and come back to life for a moment, thinking,

Yes! You certainly would expect sounds to be important in, of all places, the home of Bill and Gloria Gaither! "Soft music on the stereo,"—of course!—"a canary in a cage." (Wait! A canary? Where did that come from? I can just picture Bill trying to write another "He Touched Me," competing with a canary!) I say nothing.

"A tin or tile roof, or a skylight that lets you hear the rain, or an open window to a babbling brook, a fountain, a piano that invites singing." (I'm hearing the rain, the fountain, and they are hypnotizing me. I'm sinking further into my afternoon stupor.)

"Sight, smell, touch, sound, taste," Gloria repeats the list. "Taste! I almost forgot taste. How could I forget *that!*" We laugh knowingly. Not twenty-four hours ago we'd eaten the meal of a lifetime—not only Gloria's homemade wonders, but delights brought in by relatives from all over the county!

"A bowl of fresh fruit, a small dish of mints, a glass with old-fashioned candy sticks, an icy pitcher of lemonade, a bread board of cheese and crackers. Coffee!" She hands me a cup of fresh-brewed coffee as if to prove her point, and I come back to life.

We talk about other things. Children. Writing projects. Travels. Then as an *I don't know why I didn't think of it sooner* kind of afterthought Gloria said, "*Lighting!* It's the magic of any setting. God is our model! A sunrise, a sunset, or a stormy night, moonlight on the meadow, the light seen on an English rape field or a Nebraska field of milo. The gray overcast of a misty New England morning.

Don't overlook lighting possibilities: candles, soft pink bulbs in living room lamps, floor lamps that focus upward onto subtle shades of cream and white ceiling moldings, art lights on paintings, indirect lighting, track lighting that can be focused on special floral arrangements, on piano music, or on a grandfather clock. Many a mood has been destroyed or thwarted by glaring, insensitive light. We head out with our husbands to an Indiana Pacers game.

On Saturday morning we decide to go shopping, and on the way to the car, Gloria decides to spiffy the area beneath the grape arbor. At her kitchen door, she sweeps the big whetstones clean of the pea gravel that fills in the cracks around them.

"You know the welcome really begins in the driveway. Tell your readers to give attention to the walkway, the doorway, and the entry hall. Your embrace begins before you open the door to your house." She stops to straighten the tall array of bittersweet stuck into a fat wad of corn stalks.

"Put a seasonal welcome on the door and on the front porch, a big urn of marigolds in the summer, a basket of dried hydrangea in the fall, a heart wreath of grapevine woven with pink and red roses and ribbons on your February door. An outdoor nativity with real straw and special lighting for Christmas. Or how about a big snowman with a red scarf by the front porch?"

"How about an ax artistically wedged into a woodpile?" I say, noticing that the woodpile with the *artistically wedged ax* is greatly depleted from yesterday.

"How 'bout that it's stacked handily by the door, so it's not only nice to look at, but useful as well?" (If nothing else, I'm observant.)

"How about pumpkins and gourds displayed in a small rusted wagon at Thanksgiving?" I say, picking up a stray gourd and placing it back on top of the mound in the wagon.

"It's about *making provision for people!* That's all it is," Gloria says as we drive to Muncie to visit a little store we like there.

After I was back in Nashville (trying to work some light blue into my gypsy-ish color scheme), a note came from Gloria. A list. No explanation, just a list.

❦   Have a basket of toys or a small table and chairs for little people.

♥ Put out a 1,000 piece puzzle on a dining room table. (Author's note: *A 500 piece one is fine!*)

♥ Put easy-play music on the piano.

♥ Make books a part of every grouping and arrangement.

♥ Hang baskets where they can be easily accessible—for gathering apples or pine cones, picking flowers, gathering vegetables.

♥ Put out clay, color crayons and paper, games, pick-up sticks. Anything that invites conversation or helps build comfortable community.

♥ Have "comfort foods" handy: popcorn, soup mixes, cheeses and vegetable sticks, hot chocolate, refrigerated cookie dough, and salad fixin's.

♥ Cook something! The smells are sure to make you feel like you're expected!

Did I tell you Gloria is passionate about the subject? Do you think there is *anything at all* here you can use? *Anything?*

Chapter Ten

Look Around You.
There's a Circus Going On!

Fall is my favorite time of year. I love it when the leaves change colors to create a masterpiece of wonder! In grade school we learned the scientific reasons for this phenomenon. We heard about *photosynthesis*. And *senescence*. And *carotenoid*. How sunlight is converted into food for the trees and how there are different pigments in the leaves that react to nature's acid and alkaline—that it's chlorophyll that makes them green (Wait! Isn't that what makes teeth white? I'm confused). I don't really need to know *why* they change, I just need to know it happens!

In my opinion, it was and is information overload. Couldn't the science teacher simply say, *God did this serendipitous thing with natural chemicals to produce the various colors, and there's a reason for every shade of green, red, yellow, and orange. I'd tell you more, but by the time you're forty you'll forget.* Which is exactly what happened to me.

I'm somewhat lethargic in the summer months, but in the fall I come alive. For me autumn heralds a new beginning. It makes me think of my first year in college, of riding the train overnight to New York City—sleeping in a cozy compartment, and having breakfast in the dining car. It reminds me of bursting out of

Pennsylvania Station and being bombarded by the sounds and smells of Manhattan—remembering how scared I was, but how very brave I felt in making the connection to a second train at New York Central Station to take me to a campus an hour north in Briarcliff Manor.

Fall was never so beautiful as it was that first year in New England. I was newly in love with anything that got in my way. The mirrors in the elegant dining room that reflected my joy, the long scenic hill to the music building, big piles of leaves in which to tumble, and the smell of burning leaves. Football games, and the cute music major from South Bend who seemed to always be next to me in the mirror, and who made the long hill to the music building memorable with innocent playfulness. I can't seem to muster any regrets from that piece of my life, except to say (and it must prove I'm getting old!), *Oh, how I miss the smell of burning leaves!* I feel as though I've been robbed of a sensory high because of the ordinances that have been passed (it falls into a category called *progress*) to prohibit burning.

Gloria Gaither has described fall as the *circus of autumn.* I wish I'd said that! It's the perfect description for this stunningly beautiful and vibrant time of year. As a traveler these days, I've had the good fortune to witness autumn repeating itself over and over. Long before a change in the air has even been hinted in Tennessee, I've peeked from airplane windows—flying over Michigan, Ohio, West Virginia, and Pennsylvania—and held my breath at the giant tapestry of color that falls into glorious patterns and covers the earth beneath me.

On the ground up close, it's even more magnificent! There, the raging colors provide a showcase for real life, framing and providing a background for the most serendipitous of scenes. City folk in richly-hued fall wardrobe (oh, the feel of suede, and velvet, against the skin!), moving like machinery in nursery-planted, foliage-intense office parks, designed by architects who cared not a whit about the environment, only about *politically correct.* Families in bright sweaters in front yards with rakes in hand, or on porches carving pumpkins and hanging ghosts and goblins for Halloween. (I'm remembering the time on our own porch, when our pumpkin was so big Wayne had to use the electric drill to carve out its face!)

Pumpkins? What was God thinking when he made pumpkins? Did he picture them on front porches, with eyes, nose, and mouth? I'm not sure. Made into perfect pumpkin pies? Yes, without a doubt! Like the ones mother made. From scratch, with generous rings of brown sugar and pecans and served with freshly whipped cream.

God just had to have known that one day when I was driving across Pennsylvania, I'd practically wreck my rental car admiring the scene he'd painted: pumpkins still on the ground—snug in the husks of their basket-like cradles—against a backdrop of ruddy copse, highlighted by the touch of his brush strokes, the exact color of the pumpkins!

Running almost parallel to the highway, God had arranged for there to be a dirt road with Amish buggies, pulled by sturdy gray workhorses and driven by white-shirted, black-suspendered, men. On their heads sat wide-brimmed hats pulled purposefully low as if to block the vision. Perhaps to set the eyes against some modern convenience along the way—like a big green John Deere tractor, for instance. And *have you ever in your life* seen a big green John Deere tractor posing against a copse of fall colors?

By taking a walk and letting yourself fall in love with nature all over again, you are opening your heart to sheer joy! God's scenes of nature—*and human nature*—are far more artistic and serendipitous than we could ever dream up ourselves. Open your eyes to the circus! It's all around you!

My Mama's Punkin' Pie Recipe

❦ *(This is a secret family recipe, so please keep it to yourself!)*

- Make the crust as you usually do. This filling deserves only the best crust; my mama would spin in her grave at the thought of one that's pre-made. If you absolutely must use one already prepared, the one in the dairy case is best.

- The following mixture will fill 3 large, or 4 small, pie shells. You can keep it in the refrigerator and bake one pie at a time. Pie shells should be unbaked.

    Mix together and beat well:

    2 cans pumpkin

    2 ¼ c. sugar

    1 t. salt

    2 T. flour

    2 t. cinnamon

    3 t. pumpkin pie spice

    1 t. ginger

    4 egg yolks

    Add 1 qt. of hot milk

    Fold in 4 beaten egg whites

- Bake in hot oven (400°) 10 minutes, then turn to moderate temperature (375°) and finish. Total approx. 45 minutes.

- Ring this next mixture around the edge 15 minutes before the pie is done cooking, after it is well set:

    1 c. chopped pecans

    ½ c. brown sugar

    ¼ c. melted margarine or butter

Chapter Eleven

A Party Begins in the Heart of a Child with a Good Imagination

Long after my brothers and I quit believing in Santa Claus, we would say ". . . but don't let Mother know. She still believes!" As nearly as we can figure, she went to her grave believing in Santa. And yes, she (and we) believed in Jesus! And (surprise! surprise!) we all knew the difference between pretend and real.

Make believe is a wonderful mind-expanding thing. Everyone doesn't agree. When my girls were little they played with another set of sisters who lived in our neighborhood. One day the children showed up wearing big white fluffy fur hats.

"Oh my goodness," I said, "you have marshmallows on your heads!" to which the older girl responded belligerently, "We do not have marshmallows on our heads! That is a lie! We have hats on our heads!" It seems the parents didn't approve of teasing and were worried that their children wouldn't be able to tell fact from fiction and that it might confuse them as to the truth of Jesus. *They might think he is make believe,* they reasoned, and were taking no chances.

Barry and Sheila's son, Christian, is a child who is encouraged to use his imagination, and Sheila says it's not unusual for the two of them to spend the day as storybook characters or mythical people from literature: Peter Pan and Wendy, the Scarecrow and Dorothy, Batman and Batgirl, Sleeping Beauty and the Prince, or Flash Gordon and Deborah. Christian's parents have no idea where the name Deborah came from; apparently he just decided that he would be likely to rescue someone with that name.

When their fish Red died, Barry and Sheila told Christian that Red went off to New York to star in the circus. The fish even wrote them a letter saying how well he was doing there. Their friends have picked up on the fun too. After a visit to the Big Apple, they reported back that they were able to take in one of Red's performances and that he's doing fine.

Encourage your children's imagination. It's an obvious cure for boredom. And in case you are still worried that they won't know fact from fiction, I say they will. They'll know by your playful spirit and the twinkle in your eye. Give your kids a little bit of credit, for heaven's sake! They got their smarts from you, after all!

The next time you are part of a large

family gathering, forget the mums!

Make a centerpiece (or centerpieces)

out of photos from "days gone by."

You can showcase them in frames

or albums, or you can pile them

in the center of the table.

Add a couple of throw-away

cameras for future enjoyment.

Chapter Twelve

Unbridled Gossip from the Higgs Household

I'd hoped Liz Curtis Higgs, prolific author and speaker, would give me a few nice and juicy new tidbits to help you celebrate the daily-ness of life, but here is the problem: *Everything has been told!*

Each time something happens in the Higgs household, especially when things go awry, the whole family screams, "Oh boy, another book!" or "Another TCW article!" (Liz writes a column for *Today's Christian Woman*.)

I'm proud to say, however, I was eventually able to dig out a few little choice items for you, like what her husband gives her every year for Valentine's Day, and a celebrate-the-daily kind of adventure she had with her daughter. Later in the book, in *Celebrating the Occasion*, I'll tell you about a little Liz idea that didn't quite work as she intended. I don't mean to be catty, BUT . . . ! I can certainly see why she's never told *that* one before!

I would have to report to you that when she told me about her husband's Valentine's day gift, Liz Curtis Higgs—author, speaker, spiritual example—became slightly boastful. If the truth be known, plain old out-and-out braggadocio! I only tell you this, of course, so you can pray for her more intelligently!

Each and every Valentine's Day Liz's husband Bill cooks a gourmet dinner just for her. Before-hand he delivers a beautifully-designed printed menu he's made slaving at the computer, listing the most mouth-watering delectables you can imagine, from appetizer, to Irish soda bread (his specialty), to flamboyant dessert! After she has had a couple of weeks to drool in anticipation, the day comes, and with all the flare and flurry of a five-star restaurant, Bill serves Liz her feast! Is that the most romantic thing you've ever heard?

Dear reader, don't ask "how does this information apply to me?" Do I have to draw you a picture? Do as I do: Put a stick-it on this page and place the book on your husband's pillow. Duh!

It's a Kid Thing

Because Liz is on the road a lot, celebrating the daily moments with her children, Lilly and Matt, is important. She claims to have tried everything in the attempt to keep the connection strong. She even tried that much-touted suggestion of putting love notes in lunch boxes! It backfired, which is exactly what happened to me. Picture it! The kids open their lunch box, caring only that the food is there, and find some sappy note. The next thing they know, the note has made its way around the lunchroom, and your kids are ready to disown you.

"I've found that Kit-Kats and Hershey Kisses say 'I Love You' far better than a note!" is Liz's advice. Do what Liz does. Trust me, your children will thank you!

Taking daughter Lilly to have a manicure turned out to be another trick that worked for Liz! The two planned for it for days ahead of time, discussing what color of polish they each would choose. The day of the big event came and to say they made the most of it is an understatement—giggling, joking, and *just plain ol' carrying on!*

Even greater joy came after the fact: showing off their nails and talking about it forever and ever amen!

Sometimes in the mornings as I drive to work, I turn on country music and sing along. "He stopped lovin' her todaaay, they placed a wreath upon the doooor." Other times I put in a praise CD and sing, "Celebrate Jesus, Celebrate!" Some days are just better than others. Wonder why?

Chapter Thirteen

I'm in a Funk and I Like It That Way!

At Laughing Heart Farm, which is the name Liz and Bill Higgs have given their home, I'm told (after much prodding) that it's not all fun and games. Sometimes the inhabitants find themselves in what some would call *a funk*. How do they handle a bad mood? Very much like I've found that other people do (in fact, exactly like Sandi Patty and her husband Don deal with it): Let the bad mood happen, allow it to settle, then help the person pull herself (or himself—women aren't the only moody creatures!) back together with encouragement and humor.

I'm someone who isn't one bit tolerant of a rotten mood. My standard reply, "Snap out of it!" has been said so often that my daughter Dana (who now lives in Ohio) once asked if I thought of her as nothing more than a giant rubber band. Not long ago, when she was feeling low, depleted by the treatment she was enduring for breast cancer, she called.

"Say it, Mother! Say it!" I knew exactly what she expected.

"Snap out of it!" I replied.

Both Sandi and Liz agree, if you don't have the lows, you don't appreciate the highs.

They may be right on this one. Let's just say, *I'm still thinking about it!*

Chapter Fourteen

Starlight, Star Bright, Wish I May, Wish I Might, Have the Wish I Wish Tonight!

*H*ere is my wish: I wish I could live next door to Liz Curtis Higgs, travel with her, be her best friend and roommate, carry her luggage, schlep her books . . . and . . . *Wait! What am I saying?* All I'm really saying here is that I'd like to hang out with her in hopes that some of her chutzpah will rub off on me.

Liz and I are basically email girlfriends, having met when I introduced her at Praise Gathering a few years ago. We sign off with sappy sentiments like, "I love you dearly," "You are just too fab-oo-lous," and "I'm hugging you to pieces in my mind!" We're also on-the-run type friends, who see each other at industry events. There we grab each other, hug like crazy, kiss faces, and, out of necessity, move on—throwing kisses as we go.

Liz is fun. She's a giggler, a story-teller, and a crazy lady. But beyond that, she's a woman who knows God personally and has helped other people by writing and speaking about her journey.

Liz is best known for her *Bad Girls of the Bible* book—her gorgeous dramatic eyes peek at you from the cover—but my favorite of hers is the book I keep by my bed, *Reflecting His Image: Discovering Your Worth in Christ from A to Z.* I open it often, and here is the reason:

I have no trouble believing I am a child of God, but I'm likely to forget how it should play out in my life every day.

If you are normal, dear reader (and I'd like to think some of you are normal), you have this problem too. You get in the doldrums; you feel you have nothing to offer; you're depressed by the fact that others are more talented than you, or more attractive, or have more money; you feel like giving up! You believe your crisis to be insurmountable and that God has forgotten about you. I could go on and on!

Liz's little book of encouragement, with its memorable true-life vignettes, not only shows me that I'm way off-track, but it gently proves it with Scripture. Even the table of contents is encouraging. It goes through the alphabet assuring you that if you are God's child, then as his heir, you have entitlements. A—He is the Alpha and Omega. B—You are Beautiful! C—You are a citizen of heaven. D—He is the Deliverer. On and on through the ABCs. Buy the book! Do not pass go; do not collect two hundred dollars! Meanwhile, say it with me: Starlight, star bright, wish I may, wish I might . . . (as Liz's book says) *Reflect His Image*. From A to Z!

(*Reflecting His Image* has been repackaged as *Mirror, Mirror On the Wall, Have I Got News for You!* Both versions are available.)

Celebrating Because You Just Can't Help Yourself!

After my cancer diagnosis and during a very long and intense year of chemotherapy, Joy MacKenzie, longtime friend and writing partner, taught me how to celebrate in ways I'd never dreamed possible. Celebrate chemotherapy? You've got to be kidding! After each treatment, she would come bearing gifts.

"Time to party," she would say, "Another thing behind us!" And even though the drugs made me feel like death warmed over, somehow I'd pull myself together and open the gifts: cheap gifts, expensive gifts, serious gifts, silly gifts, and inspirational gifts. She promised a "big extravagant one" at year's end. It could best be called a "baited hook" *disguised* as a gift.

"Make it through the year, behave yourself, stay alive, don't die," she said, "and I'll give you an all-expense-paid trip to the Cayman Islands as a reward." Is there any doubt I'd be dead, had it not been for that incentive?

I frequently tell people Joy could celebrate a dead dog: I just don't want to be the dog! But don't you just love to be in the company of people like Joy? People who can't contain themselves? Who just have to celebrate? Who just have to dance, as is the case with Joni Eareckson Tada? Or fish, like her husband Ken? You'll read the details here, along with a story about a person who can turn a task like feeding a cat into a party, and another who can turn a bad day into a good day simply by thinking about her underwear!

On a more serious note, I've included here a chapter about gratitude and how it plays out in living your life. *If we are thankful in light of the fact we don't deserve a whit, we truly can't help but live in celebration!* Have you ever felt so full of gratitude that you'd write a book if only you knew how? The chapter *Comedy or Tragedy?* is for you. Kind of a writing lesson based on the principle "If I can do it, you can do it too."

If writing a book isn't your thing, maybe bursting forth in song at the drop of a hat is! Joni has that problem too and I'll tell you about it. Have you ever been so full of yourself, you've been tempted to do a belly slide on a long shiny table? I didn't think so! If that's an idea that is foreign to you, read this section and get back to me!

Chapter Fifteen

When I Think of Ken Tada, I Think of Fishing, When I Think of Joni, I Think of Dancing

Ken Tada is the fisherman of all fishermen! Not only can he catch 'em and haul 'em in, but practically before you can say, "Hold the wasabi," he'll have whipped out his knife, carved away the skin and bones, and made sushi! The sushi part I only know as hearsay and takes place in the waters of the Pacific near where Ken and Joni live. The time Wayne and I fished with Ken, we were on Lake Michigan near Kenosha, Wisconsin.

Every time the magic words "Fish on!" were shouted, Ken and I would elbow each other out of the way to take control of the downrigger. Wayne and Dan (our friend who owned the boat) didn't have a chance. Sometimes two downriggers would go off and Ken and I both would be reeling in a fish. Then the contest was to see who had the biggest salmon or rainbow—or as the case may be, *a boot,* the result of a prank by Wayne and Dan to get back at us for not giving them a turn. My fish were always bigger, of course. *I'm telling the story!*

The biggest problem I have fishing is that I have a rather tender stomach due to having had reconstructive surgery after breast cancer. (If you must know, they moved the fat of my stomach, along with muscle and blood supply, up through my torso to create a new breast, giving me a tummy tuck as a bonus . . . and oh, when the moonlight hits my cleavage . . . never mind!) Each time, before I would thrust the heavy pole into my torso, I'd grab my pillow and pad myself so as to lessen the pain. It still practically killed me!

Not long after our return to Nashville, I received a package from Ken. Inside was a very useful gift: a fisherman's belt (a fisher*girl's* belt), a beautifully hand-tooled leather belt that fits around your waist with a big cup-like thing to hold the pole. Until we redecorated the kitchen, I hung it on my kitchen wall when it wasn't in use. To say it was a conversation piece is an understatement!

When I think of Joni, I think of dancing! Yes, she's a best-selling author, having written some of the best resources available for Christian living, and yes, she is as good a speaker as anyone you've ever heard—practically a theologian! Of course, she is in a wheelchair, paralyzed from the neck down because of a diving accident. Nevertheless, you ain't seen nothin' till you've seen her dance, and I've had that privilege. I can't get it out of my mind.

Recently at a Christian Booksellers convention, with a fifties-type big-band orchestra, Joni sang and danced. If holding your audience spellbound is any indication of a talented performer, Joni might well have been a Rockette at Radio City Music Hall! She was fabulous, flirtatious, and fun! The wheelchair was practically burning rubber! The song she sang, she wrote herself.

Joni's Waltz

Though I spend my mortal lifetime in this chair,
I refuse to waste it living in despair.
And though others may receive gifts of healing, I believe

That He has given me a gift beyond compare . . .
For heaven is nearer to me, and at times it is all I can see.

Sweet music I hear coming down to my ear;
And I know that it's playing for me.

Chorus:
For I am Christ the Savior's own bride,
And redeemed I shall stand by His side.
He will say, "Shall we dance?"
And our endless romance will be worth all the tears I have cried.
I rejoice with him whose pain my Savior heals.
And I weep with him who still his anguish feels.
But earthly joys and earthly tears, are confined to earthly years,
And a greater good the Word of God reveals.
In this life we have a cross that we must bear;
A tiny part of Jesus' death that we can share.
And one day we'll lay it down, for He has promised us a crown,
To which our suffering can never be compared.

(Repeat Chorus)

by Joni Eareckson Tada
Used with persmission

Some of us grew up in churches where dancing was forbidden. That was true for me, and sometimes I feel bitter about it. Not that it hurt me one bit to miss the jitterbug contests, or even the slow dances that *could have led to childbirth* (which truly was one of the reasons given for eschewing this so-called "sinful" pleasure).

The missed opportunity wasn't the moving around on the dance floor rubbing bodies together (some of us were doing worse in the backseats of cars), but rather it was that we missed the *spirit* of the dance, the joie de vivre that says, "I can't help myself, I just gotta let loose!" Scripture speaks of it! Passages such as Psalm

149 say straight out, "Let them praise His name in dance; strike up the band and make great music! And why? Because God delights in his people, festoons plain folk with salvation garlands!" (*The Message*).

Only in a church like ours could a verse like that come with a warning: "It's okay to be joyful, but don't get carried away." A "feel good" Christianity, we were told, could lead to something dreadful. Just as dancing could lead to childbirth, this "experiential" religion could lead to . . . what? They were never quite sure! Rolling in the aisles? Pew leaping? Chandelier swinging? *Snake handling?* (The handling of snakes may seem like a stretch to you, dear reader, but to those of us from West Virginia, it's always a remote possibility.)

As teenagers we made the most of this paranoia. We sang, "We don't dance, we don't chew: we don't go with boys who do." Often on a night when there was a "mixer" (with dancing) at our high school, our pastor would read to us for hours at a time from *Pilgrim's Progress* while we squirmed in our seats and dreamed of Frankie Lane and swirling poodle skirts.

Glorify the Lord with me; let us exalt his name together.

—Psalm 33:1

It seems there were those who cared more about whether we danced . . . and smoked . . . and drank . . . and attended movies . . . and wore makeup . . . than about whether we knew God. "Trust him," they said. But how could I trust someone who is out to get me and who has a list of rules I can't possibly keep?

It took me a long time to have a desire to know God, to learn his attributes, to find him trustworthy. The legalism, the negatives always got in the way. Sometimes I'm still bitter about that, and I'm ashamed I can still get my nose bent out of joint over something that happened so many years ago. Can you believe I'm still blaming the *tsk, tsk-ers* for the fact I wasn't seeking God? Like, *I'd be a much better Christian if other people wouldn't slow me down!*

Scripture tells us, "Let all bitterness,"—Eek! Did you say bitterness?—"and wrath, and anger, and clamor, and slander, be put away from you, along with all malice. And be kind to one another, tender-hearted, forgiving each other, just as God in Christ also has forgiven you" (Ephesians 4:31–32). Perhaps getting rid of the crud in our lives and making things right with those around us better prepares our souls to tear loose. As Psalm 30 in *The Message* says, ". . . change wild lament into whirling dance."

We must not let anything rob us of our joy! So let's dance—at least in our spirits! Down a path of fall leaves. In the yard in the rain or under the sprinkler! In church (check first with the elders)! In the privacy of our own homes. In a wheelchair! Or in our underwear, for heaven's sake! Dance!

Chapter Sixteen

Feeding the Cat Isn't Something You'd Normally Celebrate. But Then Again, Why Not?

Not long after my daughter Dana and her husband Barry got their cat Puddin', they realized they would have to find someone to care for him when they traveled.

First, I must tell you about Puddin' and why it's important that he not just be cared for, but that he be *coddled*. *Coddled* as opposed to being dropped off at one of those smelly, unfamiliar, temporary lodging places with the dreadful, confining cages. *Coddled* as opposed to being left to fend for himself with a stash of food and water that may or may not last the duration, with no one to talk to for days on end. I can hear Puddin's response to either of those options: "Just pluck out my whiskers one by one, hang me by my tail from the chandelier till I'm dead, and get it over with!"

Puddin' is a very special cat. He was "hired" to do a job. When Dana was diagnosed with breast cancer, she decided she needed a companion to help her get through the difficult times. Actually, *the way* it was decided was that she threw a little tantrum that went something like this: "If I have to have cancer, if I have to go through chemotherapy, if I have to suffer, if I have to go through the valley of the shadow of death, then I should have a cat to comfort me. Whaaaa! It's my last request!"

Now please tell me what husband could refuse his wife's "last request"? And what mother, I ask, would not get on a plane to Dayton, Ohio, drive to Middletown, go directly to the animal shelter to help choose a cat for her anguished child?

Out of twenty or so cats, Puddin' stood out. He knew he wanted us and we knew we wanted him. He looked as though he'd started out white and had then taken a detour through the butterscotch pudding—a splash on the nose, a few half-hearted swipes down the chassis, and then a deliberate drag-through of the tail.

Puddin' not only cuddled and comforted Dana during her down times, but he also helped her in her business life (she is a harpist and a writer), delegating himself as "receiver of faxes." Each time the fax line rings, Puddin' comes alive. It's as though the very circuitry that brings the machine to life somehow runs through him—like he has electricity in his veins instead of blood—and propels him to action. He tears through the house to Dana's office, takes a flying leap onto the filing cabinet where the fax machine sits. He turns his head this way and that, puzzling the whys and wherefores, like "Who is this from?" and "What is this about?" and watches as paper mysteriously appears and crawls out the other end. Then he bats it to the floor where it awaits Dana's attention.

I ask you, should this cat be well taken care of? Pampered even? Yes, it should! And when her friend Lynette offered to be Puddin's coddler, Dana accepted, and I think you could honestly say that the cat hit the jackpot; it was his lucky day! Lynette and her small daughter Jeannette were already well acquainted with Puddin', having visited him many times, always bringing the most useful and interesting gifts: a kitty condo that was really a tree house three stories tall, complete with scratching posts flavored with catnip, and toys of all kinds—even one that flies through the air and could easily be mistaken for a bird were the feathers not purple with glitter.

Lynette doesn't do things halfway. She's another one of those people, like Joy MacKenzie, who could celebrate a dead dog, (hopefully not a dead *cat*). This time it was a *live* cat, and Lynette turned the cat coddlin' into a regular party. No sooner were Dana and Barry out of town than she had a picnic prepared and packed into the van along with Jeannette and her baby brother. She picked up her husband at work and off they headed to Dana's and Barry's to spend quality time with Puddin'.

Some people would mullygrub about taking time out to feed another person's cat: "Gotta go feed that stupid cat!" Another person might run by and do "cat duty" as quickly as possible: "You kids stay in the van; don't touch a thing. This'll only take a minute."

Not Lynette! She made it a celebration to remember. Her family will remember, Dana and Barry will remember, and of course Puddin' will remember for years to come.

Chapter Seventeen

When Things Are Going Badly, Think of Your Underwear

Everyone has his or her own coping mechanisms. Most of us have gotten quite proficient at the old *sweep it under the carpet where you can't see it* method of dealing with things. I once wrote in my journal, *After you've pushed your problems under the carpet for a very long time, it's too bumpy to walk on. You fall . . . and fall . . . and fall . . . and fall. Time after time after time. At some point you won't be able to get up again!*

Another way of dealing with life's overwhelming interferences is humor—one of God's very best and most useful gifts. What would we do if we couldn't laugh when things go awry? I have a darling girlfriend who understands the value of humor as a coping tool better than anyone I know. Even though I'm old enough to be her mother, very few days go by when we don't talk by phone or email. No matter what bad thing has happened to either of us, invariably we can pick it apart, find humor in it, and laugh.

Nothing tickles me more than when she shares about her dating life. I'm saving her emails and make notes when we talk on the phone so I can write a Christian Bridget Jones-type book based on her hilarious escapades. Boy, is she going to be surprised!

The problem is, men in her age bracket often leave something to be desired. The ones who have promise usually turn out to be pretty self-absorbed and are obviously (though sometimes subconsciously) seeking some mindless little twit who will hang on their every word. They are intrigued with a woman with a brain but are too intimidated to want to spend their lives with one.

Then there are the losers, and while my friend has become quite adept at squelching any possible second encounter, she does manage to keep their memory alive. That's where the fun comes in! The names she gives them (basically so we can refer back to them in a hurry) are comical. Names like Spam Boy, Dry Mouth Man, Geoffrey the Giraffe, the Italian Stallion, Baby Huey, and Holy Grail.

Because she is single, beautiful, and has personality-plus, all her friends are *possessed* in their attempts to fix her up! Even I plead guilty to that! I'm responsible for "Holy Grail," who is as handsome a man as you've ever laid eyes on—a television personality of sorts with teeth that practically glow in the dark—so I thought, the perfect date.

The reason we've named him Holy Grail is a story unto itself, and has to do with the fact he used the term on the air to describe a baseball card. If he had just said it once it could have been forgiven, but he made the analogy over and over. *Holy Grail? Baseball card?* Hello! After their one and only date, it was decided, if the truth be known, he thought *he* was the one and only *true* Holy Grail!

My anonymous friend is a savvy businesswoman. She's brighter than a klieg light and sharper than Gillette's best blade. She has an idea a minute and is a brilliant networker of people and ideas. Best of all, she loves the Lord and has a caring and compassionate heart.

In her official marketing job, she swims with the sharks, in that she often finds herself surrounded by people who recognize all her desirable qualities and use them for their own good. They pick her brain-bones clean of ideas, then swim off without so much as a burp in her direction. Sometimes after a rough day or a difficult meeting, she'll call. "Another shark attack! Is there something about me? Am I dripping fresh blood? You'll never guess what happened!"

One day she called to say she'd had a particularly humiliating meeting in which a rather self-important character had put her through her paces and embarrassed her in front of others. "In all likelihood," she said (and it proved to be true), "he'll steal my thunder and take credit for my hard work."

"Whatever in the world did you do?" I asked.

"I thought about my underwear," my friend answered, as though it was the most normal thing in the world.

"Your underwear?" I was incredulous. "Did you say, your *underwear?"*

"Well, of course. I had on my most corporate of corporate outfits, but I'd just bought these wonderful little frothy, lacy under things. To keep from falling apart, I just thought about how good I looked in them. Then, in my own warped way, I pictured myself throwing off my clothes and giving this group of very conservative people a little fashion show."

Unfortunately, by now my (former?) friend has no doubt recognized herself in this story and is dialing my phone to scream in my ear, saying I can't possibly write these things about her! That everyone will think she can't stand up for herself, not to mention the weird thing about the underwear. When she calls I'll say, "It's true. Sometimes you can't stand up for yourself. But you're young and you're learning. And as to the underwear thing, no one will know it's you. It could be anybody." We'll argue, but I'll win, and then we'll laugh like there's no tomorrow.

The point is, we *will laugh like there's no tomorrow!* I know all the psycho-babble about people who sweep their problems under the rug. I know we should solve our dilemmas, not laugh at them. But usually the answers don't come overnight. It takes time. Meanwhile, thank heaven for our coping mechanisms. Thank heaven for carpets and brooms and excuses and tears and distractions. Don't forget: A party begins in the *heart!* Sometimes in the underwear drawer!

$\mathcal{M}$ake no mistake about it: people who write books aren't always what we seem to be. Yes, sometimes we stand in the kitchen and lick peanut butter from our index finger straight from the jar; or skarf down baloney that barely made it between two pieces of bread. There are times we eat on paper plates, or worse! On paper towels! *Would you believe, in our underwear for heaven's sake?* Other times we create pure magic that even we couldn't have imagined.

Chapter Eighteen

All Shall Be Well . . . Shall Be Well . . . Shall Be Well!

When I begin a book I create files on my hard drive that have the possibility of becoming chapters. Then as I think of things I want to say, I add them until, slowly but surely, I have enough information to write the chapter. For this book I had chapter ideas titled *nature, parties, gospel music, mission statement, mundane, dance, Vestal—slumber parties, Gloria—decorating,* and so on. There was one called *gratitude!*

Somehow I never managed to come up with anything but a few thoughts: "A book with the title *A Party Begins in the Heart* would not be complete without a chapter on *gratitude.* Mention Oprah and her idea of gratitude journaling. See what Brennan Manning has to say."

I had begun reading and listening to tapes by Brennan Manning (author of *The Ragamuffin Gospel* and *Ruthless Trust*), and the basic concept of gratitude was finally sinking in. *We deserve nothing!* Everything we are and have are gifts from the heavenly Father, and we should live our lives in total thanksgiving. We should be throwing our arms in the air saying, "Thank you, Lord," all day long!

That's easy when it comes to thanking him for sunsets and ice cream sundaes and the silk velvet coat I got from my husband for Christmas, but what about the unanswered prayer? What about thanking him when I'm dying inside (me, the party girl!) and no one seems to notice, much less care? What about when I'm grieving for losses that should never have been and feel I can't hold up much longer? Brennan Manning writes,

> To be grateful for an unanswered prayer, to give thanks in a state of interior desolation, to trust in the love of God in the face of the marvels, cruel circumstances, obscenities, and commonplaces of life is to whisper a doxology in darkness.

"Whisper a doxology in the dark?" I asked myself. "You've gotta be kidding! This is too much to deal with," I finally decided. "I'll simply push the delete button and be done with it."

About that time I received an awesomely written letter from my friend April Carlson. While it didn't answer my soul-wrenching questions, it did show me how simple gratitude plays out in daily life. With her permission, I'm passing on her beautifully crafted offering . . . with the thought that anyone who writes so beautifully should be the author of her own books. I'm also reminding you to journal your own expressions of thankfulness and suggesting that you join me in keeping an open mind about that ultimate step of gratitude—to be able to "whisper a doxology in darkness."

Surely, I am thankful that one day ALL shall be well,
and all shall be well and all manner of
things shall be well.
Julian of Norwich 12th Century

December 2000
Dear Family and Friends,

Oprah Winfrey challenges her constituents to write a gratitude journal . . . no complaints allowed! In the midst of this world's uncertainties . . . when we stand poised upon the precipice of what we cannot know . . . the following vignette is a picture/memory for which I am profoundly grateful.

This is the story of a simple walk on a day in late autumn. It's Jack and Robbie (each six), Hayden (five), and I who take off across the fields and woods near our house. The day is raw with spurts of spitting rain. Clouds scud furiously above us. The wind is high. All the colors of the field blend in subtle, nearly monochromatic grays and taupes and tans . . . the glory of golden rod reduced to benign beige . . . earth and sky all of a piece. Our first task is to find a natural path through the thick stand of crisp head-high queen anne's lace and shoulder-high grasses . . . burrs at their bases. We know deer inhabit this territory for we see their droppings. We can detect where they sleep by large areas of grass matted down. We know, too, that deer make "deer paths" of their own which should take us through the underbrush neatly.

We are in high spirits. The boys dash ahead along the deer path we find. They are still *little boys*, low to the ground. They run hard. Their coats are unzipped now, their cheeks scarlet. Burrs stick to the woolly parts of their coats, their socks. They are exuberant and sweetly curious. We all stop to see a hawk circle, circle above us. We are very still. We listen to the sounds of the world. We are far away from city noises so if we are quiet we can hear the trees creak as their branches rub together in the woods to our left. Hearing these eerie squeaks, Hayden announces he'd like to go home. I encourage him to stick with it. After all, our goal is the river. We continue. Each boy wants to be leader. Robbie says, "Sure Jack . . . you can be leader now." My heart warms at his kindness.

We near the river. Here the field is full of milkweed pods . . . some hollow, emptied of their splendid silken cache. Others are ripe for the picking . . . full . . . like dozens of gossamer matches, their brown heads lined up neatly in the security of the pod. The boys and I break open these wondrous works of natural art and watch the silk twirl away in the rising wind. We could do this forever. It's only the river that beckons us away! As we bushwhack toward this destination Jack shows me what he's got. He's clutching a handful of milkweed seeds visible through the corners of his little fist. "Ami, I'm going to plant these seeds in your garden." Then "It's lookin' kinda *bleak*," he shouts over the wind. (I smile to myself at his well-chosen word, "bleak" at age six!)

We're there. Below the bridge the river runs dark, fast, colorless. Hayden is glad we're there so he can skip stones, throw rocks. But Robbie and Jack have found a strange tree . . . nearly bent in two with a secret hiding place in its twisted trunk. It's very large and very old and good for climbing too. I think to myself, "We *could* stay here forever."

But of course, we can't . . . stay forever. We've been gone a long time. The rain is turning to sleet. We're suddenly hungry and home seems far away. We take the Prairie Path back, it's more direct. I lag behind and watch as the three little-boy-grandchildren of mine . . . three little cousins, at one point place their arms around each others' shoulders. Buddies for all time.

When I was a child I used to squint my eyes on car trips to avoid seeing the clear outlines of telephone wires against the sky. I wanted to pretend the fields and streams and hills and mountains were as God created them . . . unmarred by signs of civilization. There are places in the forest preserve beyond our home where only geese fly in "v's" across the sky . . . where it appears the gently-rolling knolls are endless as are the woods beyond them . . . and where for one perfect afternoon three boys and their "Ami" taste a bit of the beautiful world as it was meant to be . . . nothing "virtual" about it.

Not long ago I asked a friend of mine, "what can I pray for you?" "Pray for steadiness," she answered. I observe that in this SEASON of Wonder, Hope, and Joy the sad realities of our lives are rendered even sadder by promised expectation. *We do need steadying.* Can we journal our gratitude on paper or write it upon our hearts? Can we steady each other with our eyes . . . with expressions of grateful love? *We do need steadying.* These words steady me:

> For I know the plans I have in mind for you,
> says the Lord, plans for your welfare, not for woe!
> Plans to give you a future full of hope.
>
> —*Jeremiah 29:11*

Today the fields beyond our house are glistening with a foot of fresh snow . . . a trillion diamonds for the taking. Beneath the snow are the diminished carcasses of golden rod, queen anne's lace, milkweed pod. Invisible within the heart of each plant, though dormant, are seeds of renewal, seeds of promise, seeds of fruition . . . completion . . . HOPE! We claim, with gratitude, for us, for YOU, even within the "winter" our lives . . . a FUTURE FULL OF HOPE.

May the peace of the Lord truly be with you and yours this Christmas.

April Carlson, for Bob, as well . . .
(Used with permission.)

Chapter Nineteen

Comedy or Tragedy? That Is the Question!

Anyone can write a book! Yes you! I'm talking to you! You have a story. Everybody does! Yours might be a *party-begins-in-heart* kind of story, or it might be a survival story like my first book, *I'm Alive and the Doctor's Dead*. In your heart of hearts you are dying to tell it. You just don't know where to begin. I know this, because I talk to women everywhere and that's what they tell me.

"I want to write a book. I want to tell my story!" they say, and believe me, there are better stories than mine out there.

If I can write a book, so can you. You may never be published, but nevertheless your experience can be a treasure for your family and friends. It may be the very thing that brings encouragement to your children and grandchildren long after you've walked off into the sunset to shake hands with the heavenly hosts. It may just be a way for you to sort things out—make sense of a very difficult time. My book was that. Deep in my heart I hoped my children would someday read what I'd written and know that a life-threatening illness can be managed—that life goes on and can become richer and sweeter because of the pain. My experience only became a book because my friend Jerry Jenkins read what I'd written and connected me to an agent.

For a long time I thought of *I'm Alive . . .* as a fluke. It never occurred to me that it might be ordained of God. After it was published, my agent suggested I write a devotional.

"Me, write a devotional?" I asked. "I'm spiritually challenged." The result of course, was *Duh-votions*. My husband thought up the title. Then came *Girls Gotta Have Fun,* and two books with Gloria Gaither, Joy MacKenzie, and Peggy Benson: *Friends Through Thick and Thin* and *Confessions of Friends Through Thick and Thin.*

Even though I have honest-to-goodness books in honest-to-goodness bookstores, I still have a hard time making myself say "author" when someone asks me what I do. Not long ago I heard myself say, "I'm sort of an author."

After all, an author would know how to diagram a sentence, right? Wrong! Not if my life depended on it! A writer would know a participle when she saw one, right? Wrong again! A participle could be dangling from the heel of my shoe and I'd never know it! As to punctuation, I don't quite get that either. I prefer to end all of my sentences with exclamation points! Editors hate that. It causes their noses to get out of joint; they go into a terrible twit! *They expect you to know this stuff, for heaven's sake!* I've been known to send an editor a whole page full of commas, colons, semicolons, periods, and exclamation points with orders to "Put 'em wherever they go!"

I call myself a "seat of the pants writer," but I'm proud to say, I'm learning. I have a top-notch teacher in Joy MacKenzie. Joy has written nearly a hundred educational books, taught at Vanderbilt University, and is now head of the English department at Christ Presbyterian Academy in Nashville. Since a best friend's duty is to keep you from showing up with egg on your face, she helps when I have problems in my writing. Instead of putting ugly red marks all over my precious paragraphs, she will often talk me through the egg-on-my-face situation. She can explain *why you do what, where, and how* when it comes to writing.

The other day when Joy sent back a couple of my stories, she commented on how I'd improved and how few suggestions she had to make these days. At the end of one piece she wrote, "This ending is brilliant." In the margins of another she penned, "This is sooo good." Would you believe? I found myself sobbing as it occurred to me that never in my life did a teacher (at least beyond the second or third grade) comment favorably on my work or encourage me in any way. In fact, in my sophomore year of high school, a teacher held my writing paper up in front of the class and made fun of it. I'm sure it must have been some crazy far-out idea, like cucumbers and tomatoes that talked and sang and danced or asked far-out questions like, "Oh, where is my hairbrush?" Let's face it, with a little encouragement I might have been the writer of Veggie Tales! Long ago! At the age of fourteen!

So pretend you are me. And Joy MacKenzie—teacher of all teachers, admired above all others—is putting smiley faces on your papers. Well, not really smiley faces in the literal sense, but she is praising your work, telling you how much you've improved, and saying *she approves.* You would be crying too!

I tell you this, dear reader, to say (and I repeat) *if I can write a book, you can write a book.* Don't wait till you have time or a special place. For a long time my place was my side of the bed, sitting up with pillows behind my back. Now I have a little room (once my daughter Mindy's bedroom) where I have everything I need, including a place to recline: a pillow-intense daybed in a cubbyhole that billows with sheer silk fabric and old lace.

And in case you've wondered where best-selling authors like Jerry Jenkins work, I thought you'd never ask. I can give you the scoop! I was there! Rumor had it that Jerry had built a riding stable on his property, and it was there where he would go to write. I could just picture Jerry coming in refreshed after a gallop through the canyons, tying his horse to a tree, sitting down on a bale of hay (still in his jodhpurs) with his laptop, ready to write. When I visited the Jenkinses, drove into the turn-around and there was nary a horse in sight, I saw how very mistaken I was. The bigger-than-life sign on the barn said, plain as anything, "The Writing Stable."

Liz Curtis Higgs has a special place to write, too. She has this fabulous loft that is separate from her house and decorated to perfection. She tells me that just walking up the steps puts her in the mood to write. "A little harp music playing softly, a cinnamon spice candle, and the laptop," she says, "and I am humming. Ahhh!"

Her loft was not always so appealing. It began as a nasty, dark, cobwebby space with see-through floors and, as she puts it, "firetrap shelving full of junk from two owners ago." Her husband, Bill, saw possibilities in the milieu and assured her that it could be made brand new.

Two years ago, the transformation began, and now it's a light and airy space with a vaulted ceiling, seven windows, oak floors, and bookshelves on every wall. After she describes it, she brags on Bill for ten full minutes, calling him smart and knowledgeable and even a brilliant magician!

Liz claims that the only thing she does in this seventeen-square-foot room is write. No business, no long visits with friends, no fast food meals, no yaks with publishers. Strictly for creative work! ". . . unless I'm taking a nap in the big club chair," she adds, "but that's for inspiration!" If you've read her books and heard her speak, I'm sure you'll agree the woman *is* inspired!

If you can, of course have a place to call your own: a certain chair, a porch, or a kitchen table. Dub it your own and stop making excuses!

Pointers for Writing a Book

Don't wait till you have time. You never will. Write now!

Turn off the computer screen (so you can't see your mistakes) and pour it out. It can be edited later.

Write about what you are passionate about. Don't try to think up some new thing. Say everything you think. Tell stories. Paint word pictures. Include plenty of "he said, she saids." Make things up. Quote other people, if something they've said or written has affected you.

Don't think about who might read it. Write your heart. Sometimes you have to write what is painful to get it out of your system. Some of your best work will be so personal it can't see the light of day because it implicates others. Let it go. That's what the delete key is for!

Find the redemption in your story. You may have to write it to find it. It's there! God has taught you something, he is in the process of teaching you something, or you are clinging to the promise that *he will* teach you. Write about it!

Don't ever think of yourself as a writer. Think of yourself as a rewriter. Keep going back over your work, each time moving things around, finding a beginning and an ending, categorizing, honing the continuity, fixing, making better.

Don't use the excuse that your household is too busy and that if you could just get away to a quiet spot you would write. Most successful people I know write wherever, whenever. With children or grandchildren running around them, in airports, on planes, or on a laptop in the car between pick-ups. Some even write on yellow legal pads by hand!

Two great resources for writing are *Bird by Bird* by Annie Lamont, and *Legacy: A Step by Step Guide to Writing Personal History,* by Linda Spencer.

Chapter Twenty

If You Knew What I Know
about Joni Eareckson Tada . . . !

There's an absorbing board game called Encore. To begin, the group is divided into two teams, and the object is to have your team reach the end of the playing board by singing songs containing a given word or referring to a certain category. After the dice are rolled and a card is drawn, you have thirty seconds to sing a minimum of nine words of a song that meets the criteria. For instance a category might be "animals," and you could sing anything from "Three Blind Mice," to "As the Deer Panteth for the Waters" to "Baby, I Just Shot a Coon to Make You a Warm Winter Hat!" (I made that last one up, but I'd certainly try to get away with it—that's the fun of the game!) The challenge is to keep singing, back and forth, until one team is stumped. The other group then takes control and draws a new card. With a little ingenuity this game can be played without benefit of board, timer, dice, and cards. In the car, for instance.

The rules say, "Be open-minded about what you will accept; don't forget the other team will be judging you when your turn comes." Here is what I know about Joni Eareckson Tada that you, dear reader, are dying to know: *She would not be one bit open-minded in this kind of competition!* She's the scrappiest, most competitive person you could ever meet when it comes to games. Especially when the games have to do with music. She remembers every hymn, praise song, movie theme, nursery rhyme, serenade of love, bar song, jingle, TV show ditty, and she-done-me-wrong lament known to man! When she lay in traction for months on end after breaking her neck in a diving accident, she kept from going crazy with this kind of activity. Now it's with a sense of competition that she sings more loudly, more aggressively, and with more endurance than anybody else in the room. Or in the vehicle. *Or in the state of Kansas* for that matter! Dare I say it? Dare I say—isn't this the kind of stuff you are hoping for?—*this otherwise godly woman has a mean streak!*

My information is not necessarily firsthand. In fact, it's just plain old *second- and thirdhand, but what's the problem?* My sources in this case are impeccable! My brother Joe spent three years as executive director of *Joni and Friends,* and Joy and Bob MacKenzie traveled all over eastern Europe with Joni, Ken, and Judy (Joni's assistant), as Joni ministered to thousands. They were in and out of vans, often traveling great distances, giving them plenty of time for car games of all sorts.

When you aren't playing games, Joni is still apt to break out in song. Joy tells me that one of her fondest memories happened at the end of their travels through the oh-so-oppressive communist countries of eastern Europe. They had moved about with great tension, Communist Party spies were assigned to shadow them, their passports were confiscated, their hotel rooms wired. The day finally came for them to cross back into Austria. This was before the Wall came down, and Joy describes the crossing of the border as "holding our breath the whole way."

"As the spy-towers faded into the distance," she remembers, "we came upon a magnificent field of poppies and I just spontaneously broke into poetry." [English teacher that she is, Joy often breaks into poetry.] "'In Flanders Field the poppies grow . . .'" ["Different field, different poppies," literature guru Joy reminds me, explaining that the fields of the poem are actually in France], "followed by Joni breaking into 'Oh, beautiful for spacious skies . . .' at the top of her lungs! Then with great exuberance we all joined in," reports Joy. "'For amber waves of grain,' we sang! Also at the top of our lungs!"

Breaking out in song! We should all be doing more of it! What happened to singing around the piano, learning all the words to the hymns? What happened to singing while you work? Singing lullabies to our children?

In Bonnie Keen's book, *Blessed Are the Desperate* (you'll read more about her later), she says she has come to the realization that, as one who has battled depression, she can't handle much of the evening news. She has to guard herself against images of abuse, greed, neglect, and wickedness. She says, "I don't think I was made for taking in too much at a time." That struck a nerve with me and made me wonder if any of us were made to handle the images that are flung through space, day after day, hour after hour, and with such intensity that it saturates our very being.

Perhaps we should strive for the time when we are so consumed with *something*—our appreciation for freedom, our love for God, our thankfulness for nature, our desire for fun—that we just can't hold back the song! It becomes just song after song, reprise after reprise. Like one unending game of Encore!

It's perfectly okay to serve the same recipe to the same guests over and over. In fact, what could be better than to be known for a specialty? When we visit our friends Bonnie and Bruce, we insist (I'm talkin' *scream-and-turn-red-in-the-face* insist) they serve their famous tacos, a recipe that came to them from an authentic south-of-the-border Mexican family. Bonnie and Bruce are so famous for this dish that, at the insistence of their friends, it was served to three hundred guests at their daughter's wedding reception.

Why not? It's their specialty.

Chapter Twenty-One

I Wonder If Mark Lowry Has Ever Done a Belly Slide on That Table

Not long ago on a visit to Lynchburg, I had dinner with Charles and Bev Lowry, Mark's parents. We sat in the big rocking chairs on the Cracker Barrel front porch and played catch-up on each others lives while we waited for a table. After dinner this hospitable twosome took me on a tour of the town, followed by a visit to the local ice-cream parlor. We sat on stools at the counter and slurped our ice cream while exchanging pleasantries with the kids behind the counter. Apparently the Lowrys go there often. It reminded me of the TV show *Cheers*, in that they all knew each other's names.

We ended the evening at the one-hundred-year-old Lowry home—not a mansion, just a big old comfortable house. The first thing that caught my eye as we walked into the great room was the longest, shiniest table I'd ever seen short of the White House! No centerpiece, no candles. Just table! Bev tells me it's nineteenth-century English, that they purchased it from a doctor in northern Virginia, and that she and Charles love the fact that everyone in the family can gather around it—grandchildren included—and still have room for more. The conversation around it, she tells me, often has to do with Scripture.

"We all love to talk about things that are not spelled out perfectly in the Bible," she says. "Of course, if God thought those things were that important, he probably would have made them clear," she adds. I can just hear those heated discussions—*good healthy arguments even!*

I can picture Bev teaching her Bible study there, or surrounded by students, ideas bouncing like beach balls. I can imagine photos spread out for scrapbooking and framing. The walls are covered with collages of cozy family pictures, and Bev tells me that when they build a new home, which they are planning to do, she wants fewer windows so she can have more wall space for pictures. Obviously this family is into keeping a record of their lives via photos. (Have you checked out Mark's visually intense website lately?)

It also dawns on me that a very long table is a good thing to have. It's good not to cover it with a big overdone silk flower centerpiece and those ceramic pottery fakes that are supposed to look like seven-layer cakes—with long-stemmed cherries on top and perfectly browned lattice-work pies—*and don't!*

One thing is certain: There's plenty of room for a lot of bodies around that table, with a turkey on each end and all the trimmings in between! Or better yet, Bev Lowry's famous Mexican specialties! My mind can only guess the raucous times had there. Knowing Mark is the poster child for ADD, can't you just imagine the dynamics at that table? It would be like watching a dozen ping-pong balls bouncing from ceiling to table, to floor to table, and back again!

Another thing that dawns on me is that I've been privileged to visit the sacred site of many a good belly slide. I'll have to admit my first thought when I walked into that room and saw that table was, *If given a chance, if Bev goes to the bathroom or disappears to make tea, I'll stand back, take a flying leap and* . . . never mind!

Section Four

Celebrating the Unexpected!

Not everyone is keen on surprises, and sometimes there are reasons why! I'll never forget going to a birthday party once where the guest of honor had been told by her husband, while they were walking up their front walk after work, to hurry and change clothes and he would take her to a special place for her birthday. Little did she know that we, her friends, were waiting in the living room to surprise her. Also little did anyone know that as she walked up the steps to their second-floor apartment, she was unbuttoning her blouse, or that at the exact moment she would be entering the room, she would be flinging her blouse in the air. It was more surprise than *any one* of us bargained for!

Whether or not you like surprises, let's face it, life is full of them, and perhaps it's best to sit back, and if at all possible, enjoy them. Sometimes you work toward some goal for months on end, and everything goes wrong. Other times, a last-minute plan turns out just right, like the last-minute wedding we had at our house one Saturday morning, or my *not-on-the-itinerary* trip to Mexico. You'll read both of these adventure stories in this next section.

Tanya Goodman Sykes creates her own unexpected moments.

Unexpected, that is, for her husband, as reported in *An Unreported Kidnapping*. What she has planned in the future for her daughters is an idea you can use right now.

God's surprises are the best surprises of all. Like for me to have the opportunity to write children's books. Something I'd never dreamed of doing in a million years. And the way God nudged me into writing a mission statement and how it played out my life. Or the surprise journey God had in store for Bev Lowry, Mark's mom. It's chronicled here, as is her recipe for fajitas! She went from being the best fajita maker in town to . . . well, you'll just have to read it to find out!

My last "celebrating the unexpected" story, the best one of all, is about my visit with Dianna and Jerry Jenkins. It shows how hard we try to make things happen—on our own controlling, manipulating terms—when what God has in store is far beyond what we could think or dream. Did I mention? *His surprises are the best surprises of all!*

Chapter Twenty-Two

You Bring the Groom and I'll Bring the Cake

One Friday morning, Sandy, one of our employees, tiptoed into my office and shut the door. Self-consciously, she hung her head and covered her mouth with her hand, mannerisms we'd come to expect.

"I need to tell you something," she whispered. "Jake and I are going to get married tomorrow." She glanced up to check out my response.

"A wedding!" I enthused, just waiting for my invitation.

"We really want to please God, but we can't wait to be together. We don't have any money, though. You know Jake's been in prison for possession, but that's good, because he found the Lord there, and I found the Lord too. I know this isn't the right way to do it, but we're going to a Justice of the Peace, just the two of us, and I thought you should know." Her words poured out followed by a big *I'm-glad-I-got-that-over-with* sigh.

"Monday I'll be a married lady," she added happily.

When Sandy first interviewed with us, she broke every rule in the book. She was the "how not to" in the human resources hand-book. She told us every negative thing about herself she could think of: She didn't look good, her teeth were bad, the only clothes she owned were worn-out jeans and a few T-shirts. With that introduction, most applicants would quickly be shown the door.

"I'll be real good in the back room. I know how to work, but don't bring me out when clients are around," she said. "I don't look good, and I don't talk good," she repeated. "And even if I could afford to buy clothes, I wouldn't know where to begin. I always just wore what was left over." Then, as though realizing that an explanation might be in order, she described her upbringing. Life in a small impoverished Tennessee town, umpteen brothers and sisters, a father long-gone, and a mama who supported the large family by working in a boot factory.

When her story was finished, she heaved another glad-I-got-it-over-with sigh, looked me straight in the eye, and with the look of an angel added, "We didn't know we were poor, but we were. We just had a lot of love to make up for it."

What we needed at that point in our business was a Sandy. We hired her! In the film and video business, anyone and everyone who walks through the door (usually straight from a college course in communications) is a self-proclaimed producer looking for a high-visibility position that pays a lot of money. We needed a *worker bee* and Sandy turned out to be a great employee. She was a fast learner, was quick as a flash, had an endearing manner, and we loved her. We knew all about her boyfriend—that he'd been in prison and had come out reformed—but we weren't aware of the seriousness of their relationship.

"Congratulations, Sandy!" I said, "It sounds like you're doing the right thing. Is there any way we can help?" As I said the words, my mind began to race like a horse at the Kentucky Derby.

"Oh heavens no!" she said. I could sense her embarrassment and her need to disappear to the back room.

"Do you wish you could have a real honest-to-goodness wedding?"

I asked. By this time a plan was working in the back of my mind, and the poor girl had no choice but to humor me.

"Well, everyone dreams of a wedding with a dress and a cake, but in our family . . ." her voice trailed off, ". . . no one has ever had one. Everybody just goes to the J.P."

"Sandy, you're going to have a wedding," I said. "I'm not sure where or how, but every girl needs a wedding."

Not much work got done at Dynamic Media that day, unless you call planning a wedding work! Before the day was over the plan was in place. The nuptials would take place in our family room, our daughter Dana would play the harp. Our daughter Mindy was given a fist full of money and sent off to purchase paper plates, cups, and napkins. Wayne was on the phone arranging for flowers and candelabra, and my assistant, Mel, ran home to get her wedding dress, which turned out to be the perfect size. One of the guys reserved the honeymoon suite at the Marriott and took up a collection to pay for it. Jim, our chief photographer, loaded his bag with cameras and film.

> If you are lucky enough to have it, use your china, crystal, and linens lavishly. Get a grip! The Queen of England is never coming to your house! Whatever are you waiting for?

One of our freelance script writers, who just happened to drop by that day, caught the spirit. The next thing we knew she was on the phone cajoling some temperamental wedding cake designer into doing a rush job.

"I know you only work by appointment! I know how truly fabulous your cakes are. I know they are a work of art. I know you take orders months in advance, but how could I have called you sooner? The wedding was only planned five minutes ago!" We were bent double listening to this one-sided conversation.

The next day, our house looked prettier than it ever had before. The family room looked like a small chapel and the dining room table was exquisite, with flowers, finger sandwiches, crackers and dips, and the prettiest cake you ever laid eyes on. And even though color wasn't discussed, everything matched as though we'd planned it for weeks on end.

Later, Sandy's family arrived in several very old and rusted-out cars, and it was obvious they had strained to "dress for the occasion." About twenty of her relatives were there, albeit very self-conscious and embarrassed, but also obviously there to enjoy the moment.

Our entire staff of about fifteen was there—it was festively crowded. There were tears of joy on many of our faces as her pastor, from a small country church, performed the ceremony.

It was a joyous occasion—a day we'll all remember for the rest of our lives. The greatest joy of all was to see the happiness in the tear-filled eyes of Sandy's mother and to hear her say, "I never in all my life dreamed that any of my girls would ever have such a day as this."

During that simple ceremony, I couldn't help but think of the day we'll be part of a great wedding feast—a party in heaven—God has spent all eternity planning for his own bride! And you know what, dear reader, we don't do anything to deserve such a celebration. He just wants to do it because he loves us!

Who says you have to wear yourself and everyone else out planning a wedding? Just do it!

Quick Recipes for a Buffet Party

(Remember, a buffet can be served on an ironing board!)

This first recipe comes from my good friend Carlana Moscheo; however, it's not by any stretch her best! Her best is for spaghetti, a recipe that originated with her ex-mother-in-law. (Moscheo, get it?) It's a crowd thing—she cooks it in the biggest pots you've ever seen! When word gets around that Carlana is cooking spaghetti, people seem to invite themselves. I would be happy to pass that recipe along to you, dear reader, but do you think she's about to give it out even to her best friends? She won't even relinquish the name of her source for sausage. Some have suggested she just might be making deals with the mafia. Her ♥ **Hot Virginia Dip** recipe will have to do for now.

- Saute 1 c. chopped pecans in 2 t. margarine. Set aside.
- Mix together and put into a heat-safe container:
- 5 oz. chopped beef
- 16 oz. cream cheese
- 4 T. milk
- 1 c. sour cream
- Garlic to taste
- 4 t. minced onion
- Half of the pecan mixture
- Add the other half of the pecan mixture to the top, bake for 20 minutes at 350° and serve with Triscuits.

♥ **Spinach and/or Artichoke Dip** is something I make often for our Sunday night fellowship group, but I never look at the recipe. In fact, I was surprised I even had a recipe. Sometimes I make it with all spinach, sometimes all artichokes, sometimes with both. I usually put a glob of mayonnaise and a few drops of Worcestershire sauce in for good measure.

- 1 9-oz. package frozen creamed spinach, thawed
- ¾ c. freshly grated parmesan cheese (reserve ¼ cup for topping)
- 1 14-oz. can artichokes hearts, drained and chopped
- ¼ t. pepper
- 1 t. fresh lemon juice
- 1 c. mozzarella cheese, shredded
- Bake until hot and bubbly. Serve with bagel chips.

Note: This is not a very colorful offering. Make it pretty by setting it into a bigger bowl and garnishing with parsley and grape tomatoes. Put the chips in a basket with a bright napkin liner.

Another good thing to serve at a buffet is salad. It's pretty, it's fast, and it goes a long way—that is, unless you add strawberries and pine nuts to your greens and dress it with this ꞏ𝑣ꞏ **Poppy Seed Dressing.** If you do that your guests might just stand there and eat out of the bowl!

- Combine and mix well in blender or with hand mixer:
    1 ½ c. sugar
    2 t. dry mustard
    1 t. salt
    ⅔ c. cider vinegar
    1 small onion, mashed
- Add :
    2 c. salad oil (no olive oil) slowly while blending.
- Stir in:
    3 T. poppy seeds

ꞏ𝑣ꞏ **Peggy Benson's Chocolate Sauce** is an easy thing to make, but I'd much rather have Peggy make it and deliver it to my door, as she does on occasion. It can be served with fresh fruit, on ice cream, pound-cake-drenched, or my favorite, on a tablespoon. In the case of the spoon, protocol demands you take your utensil between your thumb and forefinger, dig out a big glob, sit down with a good book, and slowly lick the spoon. On occasion (like every single time), you might place the jar on the table next to your chair. This will save energy running back and forth to the kitchen.

- Small bag of chocolate chips
- Stick of margarine
- 2 c. powdered sugar
- ⅔ c. canned milk (not sweetened)
- Cook for nine minutes. Serve hot or cold.

Chapter Twenty-Three

Note to Guest Speaker: Please Turn in Your Expense Report— All Sixty Cents of It!

Accepting who you are and where you came from seems to me to be an important factor in whether or not you are content. I get a lot of teasing about being from West Virginia. People think all West Virginians are hillbillies. I play along with it. I don't tell them that really my people came from Ohio, that my uncle was president of the biggest bank in the state and at one time lived next door to the governor. I let them think what they will.

"Contrary to popular opinion about West Virginians," I say, "I *do* wear shoes, my tattoos are spelled correctly, and I have my very own Spam key." (Note: A Spam key will open a can of Spam! What will a Phi-Beta-Kappa key open, I ask you? Yeah, I know! Doors!)

The greatest joy of a speaker's life (at least this speaker's life) is meeting such a variety of people. Often, after knowing someone for five minutes, it's like we've been friends forever. I just want to pack 'em up and take 'em home with me!

Not long ago I spoke at a city-wide cancer survivor luncheon in southern California, just minutes from the Mexican border. Perhaps I should say *valley-wide*, since three cities were involved and each is part of what is known as the Imperial Valley. It was a magnificent event, with a delightful lunch, a fashion show, a showcase of antique cars, and a highly interactive panel discussion with doctors and other medical professionals. The emcee, a full-time wife and mom, was so funny she could go on the road. I fully expect to see her on *Leno* someday.

Another great joy of *speakerhood* is that you are treated so well. You are the recipient of such great hospitality. I'm always asked ahead of time what my needs will be (apparently there are those who call it *demands;* I know this from having followed Ivana Trump in Pennsylvania).

"Water and chocolate please," I say, and I can hear the person on the other end of the line breathe a sigh of relief. "*But . . .,*" I say, leaving my listener hanging, "I'm very choosy about my chocolate. Not just any chocolate will do!" (I hear a gulp on the other end of the line.) "Cheap chocolate!" I say. "It must be the supermarket variety. None of this Godiva stuff, puh-lease."

My Imperial Valley hostess, Linda Cady, not only promised chocolate, but she told me there would be a person standing by to do my hair and makeup. *Wow,* I'm thinking, *wait till my friends hear this!*

"Don't worry," she said, "this person does very tasteful work; she won't make you look gaudy!"

"But I am gaudy!" I squealed. "In fact, that's part of my ministry: I have a ministry to the gaudy!"

After a start like that, it's not surprising Linda and I were best friends by the time I got there. She treated me like a queen. A hair-do! Chocolate! What more could you want? Everything was perfect. *Almost* perfect in that the bathroom ceiling in my room sprung a Niagara-Falls-intense leak just as I was getting dressed. By the way, they made me vow never to breathe a word about it—but wait! Isn't there a ten-day statute of limitations on such promises?

Before the words "I've never been to Mexico" were out of my

mouth, a trip was planned. As soon as the program was over, books were signed, and we'd said goodbye to the last guest, we had on our jeans and were headed down the highway. Four of us: Lindy Cady, the hard-working, idea-a-minute event organizer; Beverly Rogers (also an out-of-town guest), Director of Chapter Services from one of the national cancer organizations; and Linda Sanchez, who at the beginning of our jaunt, I knew only as a Hispanic gal who "knows the ropes" of getting in and out of Mexico; and me, of course!

Mexicali, our destination, turned out to be not much more than thirty minutes away, but in that short time I learned the fascinating story of the Imperial Valley. Our able tour guide was Linda Sanchez, otherwise known as the *Hispanic gal who knows the ropes.* Her official title is: Public Information Representative, Senior Educational Program for the Imperial Irrigation District.

In a nutshell, I learned this half-million-acre garden was at one time a desolate desert—that the route west to the Gold Rush passed this way and was described then as a place only for the dead. Today more than forty crops are grown there in year-round cycles, and it's become an agricultural wonder, all because of the efforts of a few stubborn, persistent visionaries, who recognized how the lay of the land—the valley is below sea-level—could work for them in rerouting water from the Colorado River to create channels and canals, literally turning the desert into an oasis.

Linda overwhelmed me with her knowledge of this highly technical process of water reclamation, yet she made it so very understandable. On the tip of her tongue were answers to my questions: How many miles of drainage ditches are there? How deep and wide are they? How do they work?

She excitedly describes how the diversions are implemented and the way the gates are manipulated to make the water go where it needs to be when. She tells me how the massive power system has been developed over the years, the outgrowth of which has been to supply power to other cities in California. She knows the problems and how they've been solved, like how they brought in carp to act as weed-eaters when underwater vegetation slowed the flow of water. Long story made short: *Linda can make silt removal interesting!*

Once we were across the border, there appeared a new Linda. No longer was she this professional person—this articulate, well-informed Linda I'd observed only moments before, though every bit the tour guide. This person appeared to be a little younger, a little more carefree. This was a happy-go-lucky Mexican chick out with her girlfriends, lookin' for fun! And fun we had!

We wheeled through Mexicali seein' the sights! From bull ring, to shopping center, to open air market, to hole-in-the-wall food stand, we experienced it all! We lingered in the shopping center people-watching and in the marketplace purchasing intriguing little mementos. As for the place we ate supper (sixty cents apiece for a dozen mouth-watering corn tortillas and dipping sauce), let's just say, had my family known, *every hair on their head would have been standing on end!*

All the while, Linda wove her personal story into the landscape of her city. As colorful as the city itself was her saga of growing up dirt poor in a household of ten children with only two bedrooms. Of a father who sneaked across the border, became a field worker, and eventually was able to bring the family over. Of a mother who kept the family together, teaching them love and working toward a better life.

Linda, as is the case with most of her brothers and sisters, graduated from college after she was grown and married. She and her husband found the Lord when they visited a funky little church where her brother-in-law was preaching. They had hoped to duck in and out (and maybe have a few laughs) and pay their respects to a family member, but God had another plan.

What impressed me so about Linda was that she hasn't let go of her roots. While the tour of the valley was highly informative and she was its ultimate representative, she really came alive when she spoke of her family. Her roots. She was as proud as if she'd been born in a mansion with a silver spoon in her mouth.

I know people who've spent a lifetime trying to cover up the fact they grew up on the wrong side of the tracks. As I said before, accepting who you are and where you came from seems to me to be an important factor in whether or not you are content, and knowing *who you are in Christ* is an even more important factor.

Chapter Twenty-Four

The Kidnapping That Was Never Reported!

It's not unusual for Tanya Goodman Sykes to "kidnap" her husband, Michael, on a Friday afternoon and take him to a hotel for the night. Perhaps it's not so much the romance of it; it's the need to *see* each other! Michael is an in-demand producer, arranger, and performer, and she is busy writing, recording, and being chauffeur to their children.

One weekend Tanya decided to do something different for a change of pace. She would take Michael out of town to a fabulous inn in Monteagle, Tennessee. She packed their bags, hid them in the trunk, and picked him up at work. When she hopped on the expressway and headed out of town, he began to ask questions. She wouldn't tell him a thing. It was a figure-it-out-as-you-go kind of thing and it turned out to be one of the best times of their lives. Time to just be together. To savor the peace and tranquility. Well . . . maybe not *total* tranquility!

The old building in which they were staying had open transoms above the doors, and in the next room there were lovers. Noisy lovers! And as they say, "sound travels." Apparently Tanya and Michael weren't the only ones disturbed by the interference. The next morning they came down to breakfast along with the other guests—a mother and daughter, two ladies there to attend a teachers conference, and a very old married couple—and since they were the only real twosome, everyone looked at them suspiciously, with knowing smirks on their faces.

Tanya and Michael knew exactly what they were thinking. But what do you say? *What is there to say?* What do you do? *You simply put your face in your plate and eat.* Fortunately, I'm told (is this good gossip, or what?), just as breakfast was almost over, in came the noisy lovers, looking like they'd been through the war! Michael and Tanya were finally able to look the others in the eye!

Chapter Twenty-Five

A Tanya Tidbit for Mothers

Tanya gave me one of my very best ideas to pass along to mothers. Each year she writes a letter to her daughters on their birthdays and files it away in their baby books. She tells them what she is feeling and what is going on in the world. She describes their accomplishments and the obstacles they've overcome. Someday she'll give her girls these letters (perhaps when they leave home for college). What a treasure! What a keepsake!

A Little Something

Paint a picture with your words
Tell a story with your heart
Sketch a feeling of peace
On the canvas of your life
Write a letter with your eyes
Look a little further with your smile
Send a bucket down to the well of your soul
And share whatever you find

CHORUS
Everybody's got a little something to give
Something to say
Don't you go believing you've no reason to live
Someone is needing you to stay
Everybody's got a little something to do
Something to bring
Whatever He gave you
However He made you

Everybody's got a little something
Is there a doubter in the crowd
You're wondering where you can start
You're saying who can I reach
Tell me who can I touch
Remember a few fish and some bread
The coin that the widow woman gave
Oh the Lord will take whatever you offer
And make it more than enough
(repeat chorus)

BRIDGE
You don't have to worry about what you're not
When you let Him make you all you can be
Even a little bit of dust in His hands
Can make the blinded eyes to see
(repeat chorus)

Tanya w/ Word/Ariose from Tanya's CD "Collection"
Lisa Binion, Tanya Goodman Sykes, Michael Sykes
Word Music (Lisa's Portion) EMI Christian Music

Chapter Twenty-Six

Old Dog Theory Proven Wrong Again!

Writing a mission statement is something I'd never have thought about on my own. Yes, I was a businesswoman for years—and I always managed to get the job done—but without benefit of a mission statement. If the truth be known, I pretty much flew by the seat of my pants in every situation, hangin' on by the tips of my fashion-length fingernails. When a job was accomplished, I'd feel somewhat surprised. *It sure turned out well considering I didn't have a clue what I was doing going into it,* I'd think. Perhaps if I *had* written such a guideline it might have been, "You go girl! Use your God-given instincts and put your heart into it." When you think about it, that isn't a totally bad idea. It worked for me for years!

Then I attended a seminar led by Laurie Beth Jones, author of *Jesus CEO*, about creating a mission statement. I was wildly impressed with her presentation, her resume, her suit, *her everything;* but, thank you very much, I felt the information had come much too late in my career to have any effect on my life, plus I wasn't in the mood to prove wrong the age-old *can't teach an old dog new tricks* theory.

Several years passed, and I had the opportunity of a lifetime—the chance to write children's books. It was something I'd never dreamed of, and when the opportunity arose, the only thing I could think of was, *writing for children is an awesome responsibility!* You can give adults any ol' thing; it's up to them to sort things out. If they don't know fact from fiction, too bad; they should stick to television! (Well, that's a pitiful attitude, but you know what I'm sayin'!)

The weight of the burden was heavy. *These are little people who are just beginning to form life-long beliefs,* I worried. *These tiny ones are their parents' treasures; the mothers and fathers will be trusting me; this is just too much responsibility. These kids are our future leaders; their future is in my hands!* Okay, perhaps I got carried away—I'm known for that—but nevertheless I was ready to back out. The burden was too great.

Then it came to me: *I'll write a mission statement. That will help me figure the whole thing out. Where do I begin?* I remembered the seminar. I remembered the Laurie Beth Jones book on my shelf.

So with the help of Laurie Beth and the Lord, I spent two days thinking and praying and trying to picture the children who would read my books.

What if they've never heard about the Lord, never gone to church? I asked myself.

What if they go to a church that tells you that there is a list of rules and you'd better not make God mad, instead of teaching you to simply know God?

What if the leaders set themselves up as the final answer and neglect to teach these precious ones that the answers are found in God's Word?

What if the time comes that there are no churches, no pastors, no parents and they are on their own? Where will they find truth? Where will the answers come from?

I was finally ready to write my mission statement, and when it came right down to it, it was short and simple.

It is my intention in everything I write, to show that Scripture is our guide for life. That biblical principles are trustworthy and can be lived out every single day beginning at the earliest point of understanding.

I intend for there to be some *crossroad* where the character has to make a decision between right and wrong. My prayer for the child is that eventually, when the authority figure (parent, clergy, church school teacher) isn't there, the child will be able to call up Scripture and apply it to life. That, through the Word of God, they will learned to hear and trust God's voice and will do what is right.

Because I believe children can grasp much bigger concepts than they are given credit for, I intend to write to that end. That would give the tuned-in parent an opportunity for discussion.

Last of all, the entertainment factor, the read-aloud-ability of the book will always be important. If nothing else, I want my stories to *sing* so that even before the child understands the words, he or she will love the sound, the dynamics, and the rhythms of the words themselves.

Little did I know the writing of this policy would come back to haunt me. There may have even been a nanno-second I wished I hadn't written it. *Mud Pie Annie* (a collaboration with my daughter Dana Shafer) is the story of a little girl who lives to make the most extravagant and exquisite cuisine from the ingredients in her back-yard. She's a child with a purpose, which is to do her best, because she learned a verse that says, "Whatever you do, work at it with all your heart" (Colossians 3:23). Here is the story:

Mud Pie Annie was a marvelous cook,
though she never took a lesson
and she never read a book.
But she had a special talent and something of a flair
for turning piles of mud into marvelous eclairs.

"It takes a lot of practice," said Mud Pie Annie as she mixed,
"And the finest of ingredients
fresh dirt and twigs and sticks
And crunchy leaves, and stems and bark, and several
    different grasses,
some tender shoots, some onion roots, and mud dark as
    molasses."
Oh, what a feast! Oh, what a meal! The dishes Annie made!
There was zesty mud-pie casserole
and muddy remoulade.
A roast of mud with mustard, dark mud pudding with whipped
    cream,
Scrumptious sweet mud custard. Double-mud-surprise-supreme!
A splash of soot, a pinch of twigs, and one more dash of dirt!
And tasty fudge from sloppy sludge
creates such fine dessert!
There were yummy fudge-crunch cookies and parfait
    extraordinaire
Too exquisite not to sample. Too delightful not to share!
Recipes from 'round the world. Mouth-watering cuisine.
Like arroz con mantequilla
    and Italian almondine
Ruggelach from Russia, mud-crust baklava from Greece.
Mud Pie Annie couldn't help herself. She had to have a piece!
Then Annie called the neighbors: "Come and taste my
    treats galore!
Come sample my new menu.
Come and have the feast de jour!"
"Just ate a monstrous meal," they said, "We're full as we can be!
Besides, it seems we've just acquired a sudden allergy."
Her mother came, her daddy too, they promised just to try it.
But just one taste of Annie's mud

They screamed, "We're on a diet!
They rushed inside to rinse their mouths and gargle Listerine.
To them it was quite awful, and they weren't just being mean.
"Our Ann could use a scrubbing—she could use a good hot bath.
Let's bring her through the back door,
Or she'll make a muddy path!
We'll douse her with detergent, then we'll soak her overnight,
By morning she'll forget about her mud-pie appetite."
But Annie, known as "Mud Pie" picked up her fork and knife.
She thought about her fancy cakes
and dreamed about her life.
Then came to mind a little verse she'd learned in Sunday school,
and making up her own sweet tune, she hummed this simple rule:
"No matter what I do in life, I'll do my very best.
I'll work at it with all my heart,
and that's how I'll be blessed.
Whether I make mud pies or great dishes for a queen,
I'll put my 'all' into it, for there is no 'in between.'
And as I work with all my might—as everybody knows—
God sees what is in my heart,
not the mud between my toes!"

Used by permission.

The book turned out beyond my wildest dreams—the artwork is so scrumptious you could lick the pages! Immediately came the deal of a lifetime. The top manufacturer of children's toys was debating putting a coupon for the book inside eight-hundred thousand—*that's an eight followed by five zeros!*—of their little ovens. We held our breath for months.

"Looks like a done deal," we were told. Then our balloon went ping, pow, poof and away.

"It won't happen," they said. "It's the Scripture. We just can't deal with that Scripture."

Would *Mud Pie Annie* be a wonderful book without a Bible quote? It would. Would anybody ever miss it if it weren't there in the first place? They wouldn't. Would God punish me if it wasn't 'there, and would anybody but me know about the mission statement?

I believe, without a doubt, that had I not written that declaration, I never would have given it a thought—I would have taken out the Scripture in a heartbeat. Perhaps the sales would have been so enormous I'd be living in Switzerland with servants in lederhosen at this very moment. Perhaps not. I can tell you this: Writing a mission statement helped me understand what was in my heart—what I believe and to Whom I'm committed—and it made me stand up for those beliefs. I only wish I'd known to do it years ago. Then again, perhaps that mission statement I lived by for all those years without recognizing it as such wasn't all that bad: "You go girl! Just use your God-given instincts, and put your heart into it!" Not unlike that of Mud Pie Annie: "Whatever you do, work at it with all your heart" (Colossians 3:23). Can you think of a better one?

Two Tips for Celebrating from Laurie Beth

- ❤ God's goodness is never lost. It just mostly goes unclaimed.
- ❤ A kite is joy on a leash.

Entertain guests in the kitchen.

Ahh, the kitchen.

Leave the soup simmering and

the cornbread in the skillet.

Say "Help yourself."

Chapter Twenty-Seven

Delayed Blessings Are Good Blessings

At one time Charles and Bev Lowry owned a Mexican restaurant; but it was before that particular trend caught on, and it didn't work out. It was then that Charles, who went back to practicing law, suggested to Bev that she go to college.

"You've always wanted to and now you can do it," he said.

"Do you know how old I'll be when I graduate?" she asked. She was forty-six at the time and had thus far chosen to stay home and raise her children.

"How old will you be in four years if you don't go?" he replied. (Mark isn't the only one in the family with quirky answers!)

To make a long story short, Bev went back to school, got her degree, and now refers to her life as a "delayed blessing." She has had more doors opened than she could ever have imagined.

"Beyond my wildest dreams," she says. "I do everything late. But you know what? That just shows that God is never through with us until he calls us home. I've had some great times in my old age." She not only got her degree but went on to teach at Liberty University, where she's been for fifteen years. She counsels students, speaks at ladies conferences, sings on the Old Time Gospel

Hour, and writes music. She made her first CD at the age of fifty-seven. Did I mention? She also makes a mean fajita!

Bev Lowry's Fabulous Fajitas

Mexican food is the specialty of the house at the Lowrys. Family members demand it! Guests request it! Friends beg for the recipes, and (please write me letters of gratitude) this time my begging paid off: I've managed to finagle the recipe!

First of all, Bev tells me, *there is a secret!* You must begin with skirt steak, which she gets at Sam's. Skirt steak is new to me—it makes me think of the Far Side cartoon where cows are standing on their hind legs in the pasture having cocktails. The caption says, "Down everyone, here comes a car." Now I'm picturing those same cows wearing *skirts!*

She tells me that next you tenderize the steak with Adolph's unseasoned meat tenderizer.

"Then mix pineapple juice with a little soy sauce and a tiny bit of Texas Pete. "Sorry, I don't measure," she says by way of apology. (Who does? I'm thinking.) She then explains that she puts her pineapple juice in a large container and just barely colors it with the soy sauce, then sprinkles Texas Pete sauce on top. (She says that Texas Pete is a hot sauce, and you can use a substitute if necessary.)

"Marinate the meat in the mixture overnight in the refrigerator; the next day cook it on the grill. Sprinkle fajita seasoning over the meat—it's a powdered seasoning you can get at the store. Slice it across the grain in tiny slices about 1/8 to 1/4 inch wide." She holds up her thumb and forefinger to illustrate. "The smaller the better."

"Have guacamole ready as well as green peppers and onions that have been sauteed together." Again no measurements.

"Oh, this is making me hungry!" she says, rubbing her tummy. Me too! It's so much more appealing when someone tells you how to make something as opposed to when they just hand you the recipe!

". . . cheese, salsa, sour cream and anything else you want to put on it," she adds. "Then wrap it in a warm flour tortilla. Mexican beans and rice will make the dinner complete. Chips, cheese sauce, lettuce . . . you can vary it each time you make it."

I'm sure I could never make fajitas as good as Bev's, so I think I'll just hint for an invitation the next time I'm in Lynchburg. If perchance I get over this overpowering urge to do a belly slide on that long, shiny table of hers—I'm making mental a note to do it *before the meal, not after!*

Chapter Twenty-Eight

If Dianna Jenkins Hadn't Been Driving So Fast, We Would Have Missed the Celebration

When Dianna Jenkins invited me to Colorado Springs to hang out (we call it play), I jumped at the opportunity.

I couldn't wait to see her new home, hoping against hope she and Jerry hadn't been stricken with that dreadful disease people often get when they decorate a new house—that strange malady that causes a person to hire a decorator and then nod like those dogs on a spring in rear windows of cars to every outlandish urn, tassle, swag, and notion known to man, throwing out everything old in the process. I was pleased to find the two of them in good health, body and mind intact, and the house, yes, with a few marvelous decorator touches, but otherwise cozy and comfortable with quilts and teddy bears.

Although the trip was planned several weeks in advance, I was excited to be arriving soon after Jerry's book, *The Mark* (from the Left Behind series), hit the number-one spot on all the best-seller lists. (All eight books of the series made *USA Today*'s 150 best-seller list for the new year!) Perhaps I'd be party to some wonderful celebration! I could just picture myself eating cocktail weenies with the creme de la creme of Colorado. After all, it's not every day such an honor is bestowed upon an author.

It didn't happen. Celebrating would come at a later date, and it didn't look like I'd be part of it. *Whaaa!* Jerry was fast at work trying to meet another deadline. Oh, the price of fame and fortune! To not even be able to stop for cocktail weenies!

We have known the Jenkinses for years, since Wayne and Jerry worked together in Chicago. Although Wayne is older than Jerry by more than a dozen years, they were sometimes mistaken for one another, if for no other reason than their girth. Of course, since Jerry and Dianna's visit to a cellation therapy clinic in Switzerland, where they shoot you full of those youth hormones, they look years younger. (Okay, I'm joking! They do look good, but it's because of exercise and diet.)

Speaking of joking, Jerry Jenkins is truly one of the funniest men alive! Because of the seriousness of the Left Behind series, many people don't know that. He doesn't miss a trick, and I like to think I don't miss much myself. There were times in our dubious past when the four of us would wind up sitting together at some dreadful banquet. Jerry and I would practically get kicked out for our silliness, always at the expense of the poor souls (be it emcee, speaker, or musician) whom we felt took themselves much too seriously. Wayne and Dianna would try to stifle their giggles, all the while kicking our shins black and blue under the table.

I arrived in Colorado mid-evening, and Dianna and I jumped right into a late-night session of "girl talk," catching up on each other's lives. The next morning, after a few hours of sleep, we headed out with no plans, but in the general direction of Denver.

"Shall we shop Old Colorado, or shall we hit the outlet mall?" we asked ourselves. "How about the shopping center with the Nordstroms?" "Maybe the one at Cherry Creek." Because we were talking a mile a minute *and Dianna was driving like . . . (never mind!),* we kept missing exits and ended up at Cherry Creek (in Denver), parking just outside Saks. Instead of going in, and for reasons we knew not why, we crossed the street, deciding on the way to have lunch at the Tattered Cover. The Tattered Cover is the most magnificent bookstore known to man. In its own appealingly cluttered way, it (all five stories of it) calls out to you, *Welcome! Sink into our deep leather couches, caress our books, discover the magic therein. Everything else will wait. Linger! You'll not be sorry!* It crossed my mind we'd spend the afternoon there, which would have been fine with me.

Somehow though, after lunch, and perhaps because it was a perfect day to be outside, we gravitated out onto the sidewalk and began to poke our way in and out of all the little shops. We tried on hats, bought silly little keepsakes, and ended up walking away from something we both wanted desperately: arm warmers! Call us unsophisticated, but neither of us had seen them before. They were made so that the very tips of your fingers would stick out. Anyone could see at a glance they would be both useful for examining merchandise and pleasing to the eye, in that you could show off your shimmery-red, newly manicured nails.

We soon realized, however, there was only one pair of these coveted little treasures left, and it looked for all the world as though *two people wanted them.* That brought about quite a brouhaha. A regular old *I want 'em; no, I want 'em* tug of war that could have signaled the end of a beautiful friendship.

At last, being the giving person I am, I handed them over, kindly pointing out they were more conducive to Colorado weather than to that of Nashville. Dianna didn't bat an eye, much less comment on my sweet, unselfish spirit. She walked straight to the cashier, handed over her prize, opened her checkbook, and began to write.

"That will be forty-two dollars and fifty three cents," the shopkeeper said, with such glee that it occurred to me that somewhere along the way she had realized they were complete dogs and they'd never sell even in the worst of blizzards. Perhaps she had been ready to pitch them into the bargain basket that very day! Now here she was lovingly encasing them in festive tissue paper and, with somewhat of a flair, was poised and ready to insert them into an even more festive bag.

"Er, um, how *m-m-much?*" stuttered Dianna in a slightly louder than usual voice. "I can't afford forty dollars for *these*," she said. (Of course she could afford them—Duh! Even I can add up the number of books sold and compute the zeros!) The woman behind the counter stopped practically in midair, almost like in a basketball game when there's a freeze-frame.

Dianna mumbled an apology, and we both kinda slunk toward the door, realizing what a spectacle we'd been. Once on the street though, we became gleeful when it came to us (practically at the same moment) that we could make our own arm warmers by cutting the toes out of old socks and creating holes for our thumbs. We could have them in all colors for a fraction of the cost of the ones for which we'd almost sacrificed our friendship.

Soon the afternoon was coming to an end, the sun was going down, and a chill was in the air. One more stop for hot chocolate and that would do it. Well, maybe two more stops.

"Would you mind terribly if I take time to run in here and get a connector for my cell-phone so I can charge it in the car?" Dianna asked, as we passed a tiny little hole-in-the-wall phone store. Of course I wouldn't mind. I was ready for us to sit a moment, and the chairs at the counter looked inviting.

Inside, the clerk, a darling young woman, was perched on a stool talking on the phone. In front of her, smack dab in the middle of her work space, was a copy of *Left Behind*.

Before she was even off the phone (she was on hold), she was in animated conversation with us, reprograming Dianna's phone, which hadn't worked right since the day she got it. At least now she knew why, and we laughed at the fact it had never been programmed in the first place.

"How do you like it?" I asked, pointing to the book. "This is Jerry's wife!" I said. *"Jerry Jenkins' wife,"* I added quickly when it occurred to me the review (although I couldn't imagine it) just might be negative.

"Of course! It's a wonderful book, it's a best-seller," said our new friend, giving Dianna a friendly once over as though she didn't know whether she should be impressed or not. Fact of the matter, she wasn't the least bit impressed; she had more important things on her mind.

"But what if all this stuff is real? What if the book of Revelation is true and it's really going to happen like it says? What if I miss it—just flat-out miss it? My parents never taught me any of this stuff and I need to find out. I'm having a baby in April and if for no other reason, I need to know for my child's sake." Her dark eyes flashed as she described her journey thus far, having delved into the mysteries of every religion imaginable (some I'd never heard of), including far-eastern cults and superstitions, in her search for answers.

We finished our phone business, chatting all the while, and as we were ready to leave I took her hand and assured her she was on an incredible adventure—that God (the God of the universe) was pursuing her, making his truth known to her; and that if she would seek him, listen for his voice, her heart search would soon be over. Dianna told her we would pray for her and pointed out to her that our meeting was not by chance—that God planned it. She took her address to follow up.

When we were back outside, our teeth were chattering, not from the evening chill that had settled, but from the unbelievable knowledge that God was at work. And although God doesn't need us—he can accomplish anything and everything without us, for heaven's sake!—he had allowed us to be part of something pretty incredible! His process!

What are the chances we would have started the day with no agenda? That we would drive past a half-dozen shopping possibilities, missing exit after exit? That we would go down a particular street, into a tiny little store (we remembered later we'd walked right past a huge phone store twice!), and meet this delightful young woman on a search for God? What are the chances that her pursuit, thus far, had led her to *Left Behind*?

What are the chances I would be visiting the Jenkinses? Hoping for a party? And find more celebration than I could ever have dreamed—in the most unexpected place and in the most unexpected way?

I'll say it again: *God's surprises are far better than any we could plan.* Or hope for! Or even dream!

Some families make a big deal over birthdays. One family I know has a special birthday plate for the guest of honor. I don't want to sound negative, but somehow being honored by a plate is not my thing. I don't want to bow my head to pray and see the words "birthday girl" staring me in the face—especially at my age! Just take me to a ritzy place to eat and cut to the chase. The presents!

Section Five

Celebrating the Occasion!

*C*elebrating the occasion is an obvious! Everybody does it! In this section of the book you'll find some new ideas you can apply to your life right now—like how you can have parties all year long and just keep reheating the same old food. And from Sheila and Barry's anniversary supper, to Sandi Patty's celebrations, to the Sykes Valentine's Day promise, to Dianna Jenkins' birthday cake idea, you'll get details! And a lot more!

You're gonna love hearing how Sheila's little boy made it snow; you'll meet Laurie Beth's carpenter who has a thought-provoking idea; and you'll get the low-down on Liz Curtis Higgs' Christmas tree. No wait! Liz Curtis Higgs' *Valentine* tree. No! *Easter!* Or was it an *Independence Day* tree? You'll have to read to find out.

And as to how the "other half" throws Christmas parties—that's here, too! There is even a song for you to sing or read to celebrate Christmas. The song is so joyful it can practically take the place of a fancy-schmantzy party.

I'm also including a story of hope from my book *I'm Alive and the Doctor's Dead* (Zondervan), about the Christmas I thought would be my last, the year of my breast cancer diagnosis. Eighteen years later, here I am! *And think about it, dear reader, who but I would be telling you these things if I had died?*

Chapter Twenty-Nine

If Nothing Else, Think of It As Saving Money

When I asked my brother, Jon, and my sixteen-year-old niece, Kirby, what comes to mind when the word "celebrate" is mentioned, they gave each other a knowing look and broke out laughing.

"Cocktail weenies!" they answer in perfect unison.

"No, seriously," I say, "what do you think of?"

"Cock-taaail weee-nies!" they say as one voice. One *very loud* voice!

"Really," I say, "I'm . . ."

"We know. You're writing a book," chuckles my brother. "But *really, and I do mean really* . . . !" Kirby takes her cue and again they shout, "Cocktaaaail weeeeee-nies!"

"Here is what is so great about cocktail weenies," says my wise-beyond-her-years niece. "You buy a big package of them at Sam's Club, the kind with red sauce oozing between their toes,"—toes?—"and you serve them at your New Year's Eve party."

"Nobody eats 'em," continues my brother, "so you stick 'em in the freezer till the next party (and the next, and the next), pull 'em out, heat 'em up, and serve 'em again."

"When your friends invite you to their parties, you say, 'Oh, I'll bring the cocktail weenies! No, I insist; no trouble at all,'" instructs Kirby. "One package of cocktail weenies can last a whole year."

My brother nods his head in agreement. "Don't even think of having a party without cocktail weenies!"

Then as an afterthought Kirby adds, "After the Christmas parties are over though, you should throw them out and start over again for New Year's."

By this time I've forgotten what the original question is. Oh yes, "What do you think of when the word 'celebrate' is mentioned?" Actually, I'm sorry I brought it up; but then again, think of it as a money-saving tip.

Chapter Thirty

A Great Idea for an Anniversary (Unless You Live at the North Pole)

Sheila Walsh and her husband, Barry, have a wonderful anniversary tradition! Or so they tell me. They pick up their kitchen table, take it out in the yard, and have dinner in the moonlight.

"It's all very festive with flowers and candles," Sheila enthuses, glancing at Barry lovingly.

"Luminaries are everywhere to light up the night!" he responds, reaching over to caress her thigh.

"We string extension cords and speakers so soft music can be played, and . . ." Sheila's voice trails off. It's like she's talking to Barry's ear. *And she's practically in his lap!* I'm thinking maybe it's time for me to leave.

Like some sappy teenager, Barry finishes her thought, ". . . and we dress up like we're going to the Waldorf."

"So when *is* your anniversary?" I ask.

"February," they say in unison, still looking into each others eyes. Then reality hits as they anticipate my next question. You can almost see them trying to turn *February* into *June*.

Dinner in the yard? In February? In Nashville? At night? I turn my questioning eyes toward Sheila, who is ready to burst into laugher.

The mood is broken. She rolls her eyes and throws her hand in the air—an *I give up, you've-caught-us-red-handed* gesture if I ever saw one!

Then the truth comes out. This memorable tradition has really only happened once. Twice at the most! They've been married eight years. I think it's like our annual Green Frog of Christmas tradition—you'll read about it a few chapters down the road—the tradition is *talking about it*, not *doing it!* In my opinion, that's almost as good as the real thing!

Chapter Thirty-One

I Could Sing Like Sandi Patty If I Could Hit the High Notes!

Wayne and I have known Sandi Patty for years, and I'll tell you something right off the bat you may not know. The fact that she has gone by Sandi Patti for all these years is really a fluke. Her last name is actually spelled *Patty!* The change wasn't an attempt on somebody's part to be clever; it was a mistake made by a graphic artist on one of her first albums, and the media (and everyone else) picked up on it, leaving Sandi no choice but to "go with it." She has recently gone back to using Patty.

Even while she was a student at Anderson University, Sandi began doing recording sessions for our company. At that time, every company president wanted one of our umpteen-projector multi-media productions, complete with a jazzy light show and singers and dancers, to kick off their corporate meetings. In the package, the "blue suits" expected a customized, high-energy theme song to hype up the attendees and tell them how fantastic they were, in the hope they would believe it and go home and do a better job, so the company would make more money. They liked to hear *"You're the best, you're the greatest, you're the hot-diggity dog of all hot-diggity dogs,"* set to a catchy tune. Not exactly in those words, but you get the idea.

We wrote the songs and Sandi sang them. Nobody did a better job. The fact she could hit high notes never before heard by most of these corporate big-shots was a plus. "I can't believe that voice!" "Who in the world is that?" "How does she do it?" "Where can I get a copy?" "Where can we hear her perform?" We had to beat them off with a stick. At that point she had done little more than sing in her home church and at school, and travel with her family, "the Ron Patty Family."

Who would have guessed that Sandi's name would become synonymous with the National Anthem? Not long ago, I asked her to tell me the story of how that came to be, how she became known for singing that song.

It was for the colorful New York City celebration of our nation's centennial, she reminded me, where she had this once-in-a-lifetime chance to sing a brand-new, arranged just for her, rendition of "The Star Spangled Banner." The project was to raise funds for Ellis Island and she felt proud and patriotic to have such an opportunity. She had no idea her performance would be televised, that she would be showcased over and over by ABC in the coverage of the extravagant weekend, or that she would be thrust into the limelight because of it.

Wayne and I were watching at home, and suddenly we were screaming, "Sandi. There's Sandi."

It was a magnificent and memorable performance, and we were touched beyond words. Apparently so was the world. Suddenly her phone was ringing. It was Peter Jennings! It was *The Tonight Show!*

"Then it was, *will Johnny Carson call me over to the couch to talk to me, or won't he?*" she enthuses, remembering the experience like it was yesterday. He did call her to the couch for a chat! We watched!

"I became tagged as the singer of that song!" she says. "I thought maybe it was a fluke at first, but then doors began to open. Doors that weren't open before." In her lifetime, she has sold eleven million albums and was one of the first to attain a platinum recording. She has sung for four sitting presidents and been featured on many television shows and extravaganzas. Sandi became one of the best-loved recording artists of all time, touching thousands with the Christian message.

Imitations sprang up all over America—thousands of little Sandis! Many a mother called record companies and studios to brag on children who "could sing better and higher" than Sandi-indisputable-queen-of-high-notes-Patti! Even I, who can't sing a lick, stooped so low as to think I could be another Sandi Patty. I can't tell you how many times I've found myself in one of those public restrooms where the acoustics are perfect and, thinking I'm alone, have belted out the chorus to "We Shall Behold Him" at the top of my lungs. And I can't tell you how many times I've heard snickers coming from one of the stalls, and had to high tail it out before I could even check my lipstick!

Life changed for Sandi dramatically when she found herself going through a divorce. As in most cases, the public is spared the whys and wherefores of a situation such as this, and never has a full understanding of the circumstances. Through her pastor and church family, she began a process of restoration. She admits to making some bad choices, but also talks constantly of God's grace and redemption.

Sandi has gone through the fire of refinement and come out restored. At this point in life, she tells me she's trying hard to cut back on career demands. (I can't help pointing out that it doesn't sound much like she's cutting back to me; she's just finished three straight weeks of concerts with the Indianapolis Symphony.) She assures me she is, that she *must*, that Anna, her oldest has only a year left before college, and that her house is a circus, and the ringleader needs to stay home.

Her house is a circus! *And there's a party in the ringleader's heart!*

Patriotism Is a Family Affair and Other Tidbits from Sandi

Long before Sandi Patty was famous for singing the National Anthem, she had a deep love of country, instilled in her at a young age by her parents, Ron and Carolyn Patty. (Note of gossip: Remember how I mentioned earlier that the characters in this book have connections to one another? Years ago, Sandi's dad sang with Fred Waring and the Pennsylvanians as did Doug Oldham. In noting the connectivity, remember: Be careful who you talk to about whom!)

Four things Sandi and her husband Don have tried to instill in their children when it comes to patriotism are:

1. Be aware! Watch the news together and learn about world events.
2. You are part of the big picture. Learn about citizenship and learn how you can take responsibility.
3. Living in a democracy is a great privilege; it's the best place in the world to be. Hold your country in great reverence.
4. You have no right to complain if you don't vote. Learn issues and take responsibility.

"How do *you* celebrate Independence Day?" I asked Sandi. "Are you so sick of showing up at all the patriotic celebrations that, given the chance, you stay in bed that day?"

"Oh, heavens, no! We have our very own fireworks in our very own backyard!" Sandi assures me. "We started with sparklers, but since Indiana has no laws to prevent fireworks, the display just gets bigger every year. We're into the high-tech stuff now!"

Sandi then describes a glorious afternoon and evening of family and fellowship, and being happily inundated with neighbors and children and dogs. And tables laden with delicious food. Then (I didn't ask, but I'm sure it must be so) she puts on her sparkly dress, picks up her microphone, nods to the orchestra leader, and sings, "Oh, say can you see . . . !"

:♥:

It's agreed upon by her family that on Mother's Day or her birthday, Sandi gets to watch any and all television shows of her choosing. That sounds like a small thing until you remember she has eight children. On an ordinary day, when she states her preference for TV entertainment, her children shout, with a twinkle in their eyes, "It's not your birthday! It's not Mother's Day! It's not your day to choose!"

:♥:

Sandi Patty's husband Don is quite the romantic. He sends so many cards she calls him a walking Hallmark store. Once on Valentine's Day, she arrived at her car to find a note on it. "Turn on the car radio and push play," it said. When she did, she heard a "life-wouldn't-be-complete-without-you—I'd-choose-you-again" kind of song.

Remember, dear reader, when I suggested you mark the page and put the book on your husband's pillow? Do it again!

Chapter Thirty-Two

It's That Birthday Plate Again!

At Sandy's and Don's house, the person whose birthday it is gets to choose the dinner. One child prefers macaroni and cheese, another peanut butter sandwiches with Oreos and Orange Crush, and another a gourmet meal. Her youngest child Sam, asks for hors d'oeuvres. The explanation is that he was always a picky eater and they had to think of something different to tempt him; so they rolled cheese and lunch meat together in little cones, stabbed them with toothpicks, and told him he was eating "hors d'oeuvres." Now it's his favorite thing.

Another family birthday tradition is to go around the table, and taking plenty of time, express love and appreciation to, and for, the honored person. And speaking of honor, when I ask Sandi if they have other time-honored traditions, I realize I've pushed the envelope a little too far! It seems they have one of those birthday plates which they highly treasure! In light of my previous foot-in-mouth comment making fun of the plates, I'm thinking I'll either have to withhold this new information or do a quick rewrite. Then I'm thinking, *differences are a good thing!* So good that perhaps we should celebrate them and have a plate made. One that says, "Look at me; I am different!" So, here's to the plates! Someone else's!

Chapter Thirty-Three

Valentine Day Gossip from the Goodman-Sykes Residence

For over ten years, Tanya and Michael Sykes have spent Valentine's Day evening with fellow musicians Landy and Joy Gardner, and Gary and Julie Prim.

Because enquiring minds want to know, dear reader, I must fill you in on who these people are. Landy is one of Nashville's top interior decorators (I couldn't even afford one of his shower curtains, for heaven's sake!) as well as director of the famous Christ Church choir. (He's the one who leads with his whole body and looks so good doing it!) Joy is a beloved soloist with the choir, in addition to being a Homecoming performer and recording artist. Gary, who also appears on the Homecoming shows from time to time, is a keyboard genius who plays on Nashville's premier recording sessions. His wife Julie manages his office, teaches Sunday school, and plays taxi driver to their two children.

Long before February fourteenth each year, this little group of troubadours makes a plan. Usually it includes a play or concert, followed by dinner at some enticing, romantic restaurant. Around the table the conversation is purposely dedicated to *celebrating* being happily married. They talk about the year, the hard times, the good times, the things they are looking forward to in the days to come. Then they make a commitment to stay married, "because we have to do this next year," which is a better reason than some I've heard!

Taking time on Valentine's Day to reevaluate your marriage (or any other beloved relationship), your year, and look ahead to the next, is a great idea. One we can all put to use.

Now here is that promised tidbit of gossip you've been waiting for: If you ask any of the six which year was most memorable, they'll tell you it was the time they all went home with food poisoning! At this point in the conversation it's good to say, "I think I'll mingle," and move on! Otherwise you'll get details, and it's not a pretty story!

Chapter Thirty-Four

Cake Decorating 101— Sign up Today!

(A juicy little Jenkins tidbit)

Dianna and Jerry Jenkins have three boys—three young men actually—all between six feet and six-five. The oldest is married; he and his wife have just welcomed their first baby boy. Son number two is in college, and the third is ready to begin college. When they were little boys, Dianna took a cake decorating class for the very purpose of making their birthday cakes. Memorable birthday cakes! I'm picturing cakes with Scooby-Doo! Batman! Fred Flintstone! Cakes shaped like footballs! Basketballs! Even hockey pucks!

Unfortunately, it's too late for me to follow Dianna's example. My children are grown, with sad memories of layer cakes held together by toothpicks and with icing dripping into their poor little laps. I'm sure they grimace when they remember those dreadful little Pepto-Bismol pink, peel and stick, break-your-teeth salutations and candle holders. Perhaps, dear reader, it's not too late for you and your darlings. Run right out—let Dianna be your shining example—and sign up for Cake Decorating 101.

Chapter ThirtyFive

Only God Can Make it Snow.
Hold That Thought!

One day just before Christmas, Sheila and Christian were making cookies. The kitchen was a lovely mess of creativity! Flour, sugar, food coloring, sprinkles, tubes of icing, and cooling cookies cluttered every available surface. Cookies in the shape of bells, stars, trees, Santas, and reindeer!

Just as the last pan came out of the oven, Christian became wistful. "Now all we need is snow!" he said sadly, as he walked to the window and propped his chin on the sill. Sheila tried her best to distract him with cookies and milk, but somehow he just couldn't get snow off his mind.

"We *could* have snow," he said, with a devilish grin. Sheila knew that grin and knew he was up to something! Her eyes followed his. He was eyeing the open bag of flour! Next thing you know, mother and son were diving into that flour sack with both hands. In no time at all Christian got his wish; the air was filled with "snow!"

Dare I ask, how long has it been since it has snowed in your kitchen? Sheila and Christian are giving you permission, and I'm giving you permission!

Chapter Thirty-Six

A Christmas Thought
from Laurie Beth Jones

One of my favorite Christmas gifts is a crate of various snacks and fruit my carpenter brings by. This year in the midst of the colorful array was a big raw, brown potato. When I asked him why the potato he said, "Just as a reminder that this is all that keeps some people from starving."

There are those who spend their

whole life holding back instead of

letting go. Celebrating is a mind set;

it's embracing all that is delightful,

fanciful, and imaginative.

It's playfulness and passion.

It's letting go!

Chapter Thirty-Seven

If Liz Had Only Asked, I Would Have Told Her It Wouldn't Work

*C*aught up in the excitement of the moment one year, Liz Bad-Girls-of-the-Bible Curtis Higgs decided to leave her Christmas tree up for the entire year. (I'm betting on the fact it was artificial but I haven't asked!) In December it was exquisitely laden with the obvious seasonal decor, and in January it was easy to create a whole different mood by simply removing the red and green tchotchkes, Santas, shiny balls, glittering garlands, and anything else that smacked of Christmas, and leaving what was left: angels, icicles, snowflakes, and velvet magnolias. Voilá! *A "winter tree."*

It gets a little tacky for my taste in March, when for St Patrick's Day green pipe cleaners get coaxed into various sized shamrocks to replace the *winter mood.* Liz isn't thinking tacky however. She's thinking "green on green," for heaven's sake!

On and on through the year: flowers for Easter, and *since that looks so good we'll just leave 'em up for summer!* And in July, let's add some of those little American flags. Flags and flowers! Don't forget, the flowers are still there!

By the time August rolls around the whole family is hating the tree. They are going out of their way to stay out of the living room, calling it "that *tree!*" Guests say it another way: "Well, *that* is a tree!"

Stubbornly Liz shops for little school bells and apple-for-the-teacher decoratives for a back-to-school tree; but when it's time for fall house-cleaning, she finally gives in. The tree comes down. The family is happy, and they are receiving guests again. I'm sorry to report, however, that when Christmas came around the next year, the Higgs family had a real tough time getting into the Christmas spirit. Putting up another tree just wasn't on their list of priorities. Oh, Liz, if you had just called!

Chapter Thirty-Eight

Think of Your Guests, Think of Your Guests, Think of Your Guests!

I hate to brag on my friends too much, for fear they'll get the big head and leave me in their dust, *but* . . . ! Marsha Blackburn, whom you've already met, is not only a state senator and a time management expert, but she and Chuck (a banking guru) throw a fine party! Each Christmas we practically stand by the mailbox waiting for our invitation. We are never disappointed.

Several hundred Nashvillians park their cars at the nearby school and are shuttled to the top of a steep hill where the Blackburns have tented the lawn and the sundeck to expand their already ample home. (If you must know, it's the old Minnie Pearl home on Murray Lane!) The invitation calls it a "drop-in," but let's face it, most people stay as long as possible.

I couldn't begin to tell you how fabulous this event is, or the luminaries who attend; but I can tell you this: Even with all the exquisite decorations, the delicacies, the finery fit for a king, you aren't the least bit intimidated. You aren't even daunted by the big-wheel, mugga-mugga important people around you. Chuck and Marsha see to that. They are moving around chatting, laughing, checking on refills, introducing, pushing people into huddles, and doing what they do best: creating a mood of hospitality.

You may never give a party like the Blackburns, dear reader: I certainly would never even hope to. But I'm sure we can all use of a few of Marsha's tips for entertaining, even if for us, it's on paper plates on the floor. They are:

Think of your guests.

Think of your guests.

Think of your guests!

*E*ntertaining isn't

about you (or me),

it's about getting

people together for

a good time.

Chapter Thirty-Nine

The Green Frog
of Christmas

More than anything that year, I wanted Christmas to be what it usually was at our house—memorable. I was determined to have an eventful, rambunctious Christmas even though the chemical buildup from ten months of chemotherapy left me feeling ugly, puffy, lethargic, and full of poison. I repeatedly had to remind myself to *snap out of it!*—a favorite saying at our house.

The doctor juggled my treatment schedule so I could finish early in December—the intent being that I had a better chance for feeling good at Christmas. It comforted me to know I had only two months of chemo to go, but there was another worry I couldn't shake.

One day while waiting for the doctor, I'd become restless and looked around for a magazine with which to pass the time. There was none and, finding nothing better to do, I began to rummage through his files. "If he finds his stuff rearranged, he'll never make me wait again," I reasoned. Then I spotted my own folder—my medical file—and began to read. Most of it was routine reports detailing my office visits and test results.

Toward the back, however, I discovered a letter written by my

mastectomy surgeon. It said I wasn't a good candidate for reconstructive surgery because I probably wouldn't live that long! "Too
bad," he said. "She is the type who would give great encouragement to others."

After I jump-started my pacemaker, my first thought was, *Well,
Mister Cowboy Doctor* (he wore cowboy boots), *I've laughed in your
face before and I'll do it again. After all, I'm still alive ten months later,
and I believe I can make it two more months. Maybe longer.* The bravado
was only skin deep; a lump formed in my throat and a knot settled
in the pit of my stomach.

Maybe this IS my last Christmas, I worried. I remembered the
lyrics to a love song, "If ever I would leave you, it wouldn't be in
springtime." The verses that follow say it wouldn't be in fall, winter, or summer either. Maybe I'd write a verse of my own: "If ever
I would leave you, it wouldn't be at Christmas; I don't want your
second wife to have my manger scene from Bethlehem!"

I thought back over the fun and excitement of Christmases
past—the year Wayne gave me a chocolate chess set, the time I
gave him a pinball machine, the year I watched two grown men—
Wayne and Jon—try to assemble a Barbie condo and never get it
right.

One day several years before, Jon (who makes pickles from the
cucumbers and dill from his own garden) discovered I didn't have
a garlic press—powdered garlic was good enough for me—and
began to taunt me.

"How can you call yourself a cook? No garlic press?" Then he
would turn to whoever happened to be nearby and ask, "Can you
believe this woman has no garlic press?"

Long before Christmas that year, I knew there would be a garlic
press under the tree. The surprise was that it was *electric,* or maybe
I should say *pseudo-electric!* Jon had gone to great trouble to attach
a thick, long electrical cord with an industrial-sized plug to an

ordinary garlic press. Had I plugged it in I probably would have been electrocuted on the spot!

Our family loves Christmas! We even love the last-minute shopping, decorating, package wrapping, silver polishing, and baking—the whole family in the kitchen trying recipes, friends stopping by for a few hours with their recipes and going home with a sampling of everything.

Mid-afternoon on Christmas Eve the celebrating begins at our house. We follow a plan, which we started when Dana was a baby, and it continues to the present time: Christmas is at our house; everyone is invited and whoever comes must *move in*—for two nights *at least.*

Most years, once our guests arrive, we can't get rid of them; and the frivolity continues for days, sometimes right up to New Year's. Once we get started, we can't stop—eating, playing games, working jigsaw puzzles, taking naps, watching movies, and then repeating it over and over. Dana, Mindy, Jon, Becky, Cara, and Kirby always come, and some years the Nixons, Becky's parents. We fondly remember when our parents were alive and part of the festivities. Now we have Barry, our son-in-law, with us.

"Trr-dition!" we sing, trilling our *R*s and mimicking the Jewish accents of *Fiddler on the Roof.*

Tradition! We certainly have ours. One of our most famous is the "Traditional Green Frog of Christmas"!

Wayne isn't what I'd call a shopper, although he's instructed, "When I die, bury me at the mall . . . so Sue and the girls will visit me often!" He loves one type of store, however—the kind that sell kitchen gadgets. On one of his trips there, Wayne discovered a plastic ice mold in the shape of a frog, so he bought it, brought it home, and acted like a kid with a new toy.

Christmas Eve morning he took the ice mold out of the box, filled it with water, added green food coloring, stuck it in the freezer, and checked its progress regularly. "Yeah, it's freezing—the Green Frog of Christmas is freezing nicely," he said.

"We're happy for you, Daddy," Mindy answered in her most insincere voice and rolled her eyes at the ceiling.

"The Green Frog of Christmas!" Dana and I mouthed the words to each other, held our stomachs, and bent over in not-too-silent laughter. Wayne was so euphoric he didn't noticed our mockery.

The "Traditional Green Frog of Christmas" was a hit from the first. Wayne waited till everyone gathered for the Christmas Eve festivities—family, friends, and neighbors. Everything was perfect—the smoked salmon with cream cheese and capers, cheese puffs, pâté and crackers, and a huge array of homemade cookies and candy.

When he had everyone's attention, he carried in the exquisite cutglass punch bowl and placed it on its fancy gilded base. There in the middle of the bright red punch sat the "Traditional Green Frog of Christmas" glistening proudly. We praised Wayne for his creative idea and workmanship and responded with affirmations, however insincere, to his "Do you like the frog? Huh? Do you like the frog?"

But the moment of glory—for both Wayne and the green frog—didn't last long. As the frog began to melt, sounds much like those of a belch—or worse—came forth from his *green-ness*! Not only that! As the green food coloring blended with the red punch, the mixture took on the color of the "or worse," if you know what I mean.

We actually only celebrated the "Traditional Green Frog of Christmas" once. I suppose it's the retelling of the story that's the tradition! Barry and Sheila know about that.

Each year after our scrumptious buffet we read the Christmas story. Then we share personal thoughts about the true meaning of Christmas, and Wayne leads us in a prayer, thanking God for sending his Son Jesus, who is the true meaning of Christmas.

I'd like to to be able to say the spiritual mood lingers, but not so. We're too wound up. We quote "The Night Before Christmas" as best we can, stopping partway through when we remember we've left out something.

"Didn't we forget the part about the 'obstacles mount to the sky'?" someone will say, "and what about 'the leaves before the wild hurricane fall'?" We begin again, but never quite get it right.

Next we pile cookies on a plate for Santa. (Christmas morning we find handwritten notes with such bizarre remarks as "Burp!" or "Your cookies made my reindeer sick!") After everyone is finally in bed, Santa goes to work—making the family room look like a window in a department store, laying the wood for an early morning fire, and getting the big coffee pot ready to plug in.

By five-thirty the next morning, if Wayne can hold off that long, we're all wide-eyed and ready to see what Santa has brought.

It takes several hours to open gifts. We do it one-at-a-time and "ooh and ahhh" over each one. Clothes are modeled on the spot. Then the traditional breakfast—ham slabs cooked outside on the grill, steeplechase eggs, my chicken-liver stroganoff, Dana's cheese grits, and Becky's incredible zucchini bread. Later in the day, after naps, we have our Christmas dinner with all the trimmings.

Savoring all these wonderful memories made me realize I had no intention of walking off into the sunset to spend Christmas with Elvis! But then again, I thought, this *could* be my last. A lot can happen in a year.

What I really wanted to do was have a pity party, but instead I had a long talk with myself. *Snap out of it!* and *Stop your mullygubbing!* didn't seem to be working too well. I reminded myself I'd been the center of attention for almost a year. Food had been planned to my liking and schedules arranged for my benefit. My family and friends had become my servants, and everything had revolved around me. Perhaps it was time to change that.

Maybe the reason was selfish—*If this truly is my last year, then I want my family to remember wonderful me!* Whatever my motive, I later realized it *was* a turning point. It would have been easy to stay where I was with people catering to my whims.

I've met several women who have never managed to get beyond this point. One woman told me she had cancer twenty-five years ago, and then proceeded to give me twenty-five years of details.

"Even though they tell me I'm cured," she said, "I just never got over it; my family still has to do everything for me."

After that I wrote a little sign and put it on the wall by my desk that said: "Dear God, please spare me from other women's cancer stories." With that in mind, maybe I could at least snap *part of the way* out of it for the Christmas season—maybe mullygrub slightly less.

Something comes over you when you face the possibility of dying. Not only do you feel a compulsion to get your house in order—throw away the ragged underwear and clean out the drawers—but there is an overwhelming need to leave something significant behind as a reminder of your life.

For the first time I wrote a Christmas letter, hoping my friends would tuck it away and save it. "Sue's last letter," they would say. I took care not to mention cancer or sickness. After all, I didn't want them to say, "Sue's last letter was a real downer. Pitiful . . . just pitiful!" Instead I wrote:

Dear Friends:

As I write this, we're in windy, cold Chicago. Once again, Wayne has kept his promise (made fifteen years ago) that he'd bring me back to do my Christmas shopping and see the sights only a big city can offer.

The snow is blowing wildly, but we are snuggled into our hotel room for the night. What fun we've had eating in our favorite places, enjoying the beauty of North Michigan Avenue with its millions of tiny white lights . . . and shopping . . . special things for the girls gift-wrapped as only Saks can do. A black satin hat for me with a veil down to my chin! Wayne carried the packages and the shopping bags and didn't grumble, not even when I bought the hat . . . only when I wore it!

It's late now, and Wayne is sleeping, but my mind is full of things I want to do this Christmas season . . . fill the cookie jar, light the hill to our house with little white lights like Michigan Avenue, and invite everyone over, especially those I haven't seen for a long time.

My heart is overflowing with joy, and I'm so very grateful. First of all, for one of God's very best ideas . . . friends! Grateful too for my family! For Mindy, who fills my life with fun and little surprises like a love note tucked in my suitcase or flowers by my bed when I wake up. For Dana, who moved into her very own apartment just a couple of miles away but comes home several times a week because she's "homesick." And Wayne, who has given me more love and cherishing than I knew was possible in the almost twenty-five years since he promised to do that.

At this time when "peace on earth" is utmost in our minds, the profundity of Scripture rings forth for all time to those who believe: "Peace I leave with you; my peace I give you. . . . Do not let your hearts be troubled and do not be afraid."

Love,
Sue

The letter out of the way, I could concentrate on special gifts for my family. Never before had I thought so diligently about what to give. I knew my sympathetic family would understand if I gave them nothing. What a year it had been with the mastectomy, the diagnosis, the aggressive treatment, and Mother's illness and death.

While I was planning my last Christmas with my family, Wayne was going through his own dilemma. For years he'd admired a diamond ring guard that would encase my emerald-cut engagement ring, and he secretly planned to buy it for me for our twenty-fifth wedding anniversary, a year and a half away. His problem was that I might not live that long. After much thought he decided I would have my ring guard for Christmas.

A week before, my daughter happened to notice I'd lost the emerald-cut diamond from my engagement ring. We searched the house over but it was nowhere to be found. "Like finding a needle in a haystack," I commented and reminded myself it was insured and it could be replaced. Wayne wasn't so easily placated. In fact, I'd never seen him so upset.

"Honey, it's okay," I told him. "We can take care of it after Christmas, when things aren't so busy." He would not be comforted. He worried about it constantly and crawled around on his hands and knees peering under every piece of furniture in the house. I could see he was terribly upset but didn't know the reason.

Four days before Christmas, I was sitting at the kitchen table with Mary Shillis, Mindy's best friend and our neighbor, when she jumped to her feet, ran to the corner where we feed the cats, moved their dish aside, and yelled, "I found it. Call Wayne!" Wayne was home in a matter of minutes, grabbed the stone and the ring, and breathlessly exclaimed, "Don't worry. I'll get it fixed for you!"

When I opened my package on Christmas morning there was my ring surrounded by fourteen sparkling diamonds. I was surprised and Wayne was glowing. Sure, he had some frantic moments, but ultimately his gift was presented in the very best possible way. I often remind Wayne that by threatening to die, I tricked him into buying me the beautiful ring and then tricked him again by being alive for our twenty-fifth anniversary so he would have to buy another present!

The dilemma of what I could give my loved ones loomed. One day as I was straightening the laundry room the answer came when I picked up a ragged quilt that had been passed down through the family. As I unfolded it, a flood of memories unfolded with it, and an idea as well. *I'll frame several of the large designs and give them to my daughters and brothers; I'll write my memories of the quilting bee and the ladies who created this beautiful work of art.*

I continued to play out the scene in my mind: *I can see it now. Someday when one of my daughters is famous, she'll be asked, "What was your best Christmas gift ever?" She'll think a moment and answer, "The last year my mother was with us she had some pieces from an old quilt framed . . ." Tears would come to her eyes and her voice would break; then she'd repeat the story attached to the back of the frame.*

Well, it may not have happened exactly as I've described it here, but on Christmas morning when I presented what I thought was to be my *final* gift to my daughters and brothers, there wasn't a dry eye as we read the story aloud together.

CHRISTMAS 1983
My gift to you is a sunflower . . . and a story

This pattern is called Sunflower, and this tattered piece was once part of a quilt made by the ladies of the Langsville, Ohio Christian Church, where my grandparents attended. My first memory of it is tracing its pattern as I lay on the daybed at Grandma Entsminger's. When my grandmother died, it was my mother's and for years it was folded at the foot of her bed.

When it became mine, I had no idea of its value or the sentiments I should feel. I took it on picnics, used it as a tablecloth, and spread it on the floor when I rolled around with my babies. I bleached it and put it through too many washings until it was worn and falling apart. Still I couldn't throw it away. The patterns were too beautiful. Maybe in this frame, its beauty will last another generation or two. Here's its story:

When I was a child, I used to spend weeks at a time with Grandpa and Grandma Entsminger at their home in the country near Langsville. Church was important to the community, and since there was only one, the Christian Church, that's where everyone went (Aunt Maggie always attended but reminded us she was really a Presbyterian since she continued to hold her membership in the Presbyterian church in Zanesville).

I was fascinated by the pump organ and even more so with Clarice, the lady who played it. Clarice had been Mother's friend since they were young girls. She was beautiful, though born crippled—in those days, they called it *hunchback*—and to me her predicament seemed both tragic and dramatic. I couldn't keep my eyes off her, and when I got home I would hurry to the piano and pretend that I too was hunchbacked!

The church didn't have a minister—at least not regularly—but it did have a choir. Visitors were invited to sing, and as soon our family walked in, we were ushered up the center aisle past the potbellied stove to the choir loft. Daddy would sing at the top of his voice; I would be more than a little embarrassed.

Quilting day, which was held in different homes, was a monthly occasion and the ladies arrived early, prepared to spend as many hours as possible. They would set up their quilting frame, drape their unfinished work across it, take their places around it, and begin a wonderful day of gossiping, laughing, and eating. As they stitched and chatted, their fingers were busy creating beautiful kaleidoscopes of colorful fabric bits that became a work of art. More importantly for them, a blanket of warmth to keep out the cold of a winter's night.

The busy scene, like a Norman Rockwell painting, is still in my mind; but most of all, I remember impressions of ordinary people creating a masterpiece.

Mrs. Laidley was rather heavy, but that wasn't important in those days. In fact I heard them say that a hefty woman was a good sign her husband was supporting her well. Laurie Folden, my grandma's best friend, was small and fragile looking. Her son was a pilot and once landed his plane in the pasture next to her house. They talked about that for years.

I remember Elsie, whose laughter was loud and boisterous, and I wonder now if her handiwork was a bit less exact than the others since she was having such a hilariously good time.

Aunt Annie's stitches were probably tight just like she held her needle . . . and her mouth even more so. I could tell from her voice she was often sad and worried about things the others never even thought of. I knew Aunt Annie's story, although she never spoke of it.

One morning her young husband had kissed her goodbye and gone outside and shot himself. They found his body by the fence. I never heard an explanation as to why, but in those days children didn't ask questions. No wonder, though, there wasn't as much joy in Aunt Annie's heart as there was in the hearts of her quilting sisters who had loving husbands to cook and bake and do for.

Aunt Maggie had an edge on the others. She'd been to California—her daughter lived there—and she knew firsthand what *they* were doing in California. She'd even taken ceramics while she was there and brought back samples of her handiwork. And of course, Aunt Maggie was a Presbyterian.

Barbara, the local beautician didn't make it to quilting day. Maybe that was good because it gave the others a chance to discuss the fact that she had divorced her husband and had bleached her hair to boot! Neither of those things had been done in Langsville before!

. . . and so, those country women and others who've faded from my mind worked together making a necessary household item. Little did they know as they pursued their routine, their ritual, that they were creating a treasure of history for us to enjoy. All that's left is a sunflower . . . a piece of history . . . and a story . . .

. . . and that's my gift to you.

From *I'm Alive and the Doctor's Dead*
By Sue Buchanan
Used with permission.

Unspeakable Joy!
Promised Messiah!
Our Immanuel!
Alpha, Omega and King!
The Hope of the Ages
At last has been born!
Let's join all creation and sing!

CHORUS
Joy, joy, unspeakable joy!
Music is filling the air
Glory, oh, glory to God!
Angels are everywhere.

Come and adore Him—
Young Mary's sweet boy—
There in the manger asleep.
Eden's deep wound
Will be taken away
By the Lamb lying there with the sheep!

(repeat chorus)

Words by Gloria Gaither. Music by William J. Gaither
© 2000 Gaither Music Company.
All rights controlled by Gaither Copyright Management.
Used by permission.

Even if your house is small,
don't let that stop you from
entertaining. Crowd 'em in.
Have a picnic on the floor if
necessary. Our best parties
were before we had furniture
for the living room.

Section Six

Celebrating in Spite of . . . !

A ll reports are in and life is officially declared to be unfair! "Stuff happens," as the saying goes. We watch while those we love do stupid things: overeat, get drunk, do drugs, abuse each other, have dreadful accidents, lose jobs, lose families, get sick, and even die.

Since we've seen it happen before and history seems to repeat itself, we worry that we ourselves might die, although we're still holding out hope for a one-size-fits-all cure. Or for a mass *fixing* from God! And in our attempt to assure that happens, we question him, shout at him, make demands of him, and superstitiously say to him, "If I do this and this and this, God, then you'll do that: make my life a bed of roses!" How long has it been since you've heard, "Thy will be done"? We just don't seem to get it!

Where is God in all this anyway? And is it possible, like Brennan Manning says, to "whisper a doxology in darkness"?

This last section of the book is about celebrating when you really don't feel like it. In spite of the motion sickness we're feeling as a result of the all the pouring back and forth that's goin' on— read about the grape-making process and you'll understand! I've included stories about how we lift each other up during the difficult times, and the words to the song, "God of the Mountain"—a song that has literally "propped me up" when otherwise I would have been a jelly fish.

Bonnie Keen's situation was about as desperate as it gets when her life was turned upside-down by divorce. As painful as it was, today there's a party goin' in that girl's heart again and God is using her experience to encourage others. In her own words, she'll tell you how one experience left her children *scarred for life!* (It's a funny story, I promise!)

Sometimes we need to take life a day at a time and simply ask for *Grace for the Moment.* I've written about my celebratin' friend Buddy Greene, and how he lives out the song he wrote by that title: "Grace for the Moment."

Another visual picture I'm pondering is this thing about God's refining fire! Is it my imagination, or does that *refinement* thing come up over and over in this last section of the book?

Then all things must come to an end and this book is no different! In fact, *we* (you and I, dear reader) will come to our own end—let's face it, the worms will be playing pinochle on our snouts, for heaven's sake—and all celebration will cease. *Or . . . wait!* Will it? Must it? Stay tuned!

Chapter Forty

Would You Say It Takes Purple Feet to Get a Refined Heart?

When you are in the middle a difficult time, invariably someone will say, "God is refining you." I've been known to answer, "I'm refined! I'm refined! Enough already!" Joking aside, I do spend a lot of time thinking about why certain things happen. Did God cause it, or did He allow it? If so, why? To make me squirm? To prove a point? To make me an example to others? To crowd me to himself?

Have you ever heard of the person who only *gets it* when you draw her a picture? I'm that person! Author Ed Miller drew me a picture in his book *Vessel to Vessel* that helped me come to a better understanding of how God works and how it relates to me.

The Scripture he uses is Jeremiah 48:11. It says, "Moab hath been at ease from his youth, and he hath settled on the lees, and hath not been emptied from vessel to vessel, neither hath he gone into captivity. Therefore his taste remained in him, and his scent is not changed."

The expression "emptied from vessel to vessel" has its history in the wine-making process. The ancient custom called for first crushing the grapes (and my mental picture says they put on a CD, took off their sandals, got into the vats barefoot, and stamped like crazy), then going through the arduous process of pouring the juice from jar to jar, over and over, day after day. Each time, there would be a waiting period that would allow for the bad stuff (the lees) to settle to the bottom. At last the juice would be completely pure. Refined.

This is earthshaking! *God loves us enough to engineer change in our lives.* We are poured back and forth, back and forth, back and forth, and each time the dregs settle. We have health; we have sickness. We have peace; we have turmoil. We have prosperity; we have adversity. Without change we become stale and unsavory. As the dregs settle we are becoming purified. Refined!

Chapter Forty-One

A Mexican Restaurant, Mark Lowry, and Possibly One of the Worst Days of Our Lives

In a video interview about this book, I was asked if it were possible to find ways to celebrate in the tough times, when you feel there is nothing to celebrate. The question threw me for a loop.

"Uh, ah, . . . y-yes, . . . uh, um, . . . n-no, . . . yikes, . . . gee, . . . m-maybe, . . . err, . . . s-sometimes, . . . p-p-p-perhaps, . . . !" Weird gobbledegook was coming from my mouth and the interviewer looked at me like I was from Mars. Then, with seemingly great conviction, I added (it was as though a streak of brilliance hit my brain) ". . . but only in retrospect!" *Only in retrospect?* Where did *that* come from? What did that *mean?* It reminded me of a funny little quip from my friend, author and speaker Peggy Benson: "How do I know what I think, till I hear what I say?"

It's okay to be sputtering like a car that's just run out of gas when you're with friends, but not when you are being recorded for posterity. When you are asked a perfectly reasonable question on the subject about which you've written—duh!—*you're supposed to have answers!* Since then, I've tried to figure out what I think—and not just because it might come up again. (Although, believe me, it's reason enough!)

I've come to the conclusion that when you are smack-dab in the middle of a serious life crisis—when you're barely hanging on by the tips of your fashion-length fingernails—it's hard to exist, much less celebrate! Sometimes we talk a good game and go through the motions; but if the truth be known, we're fooling ourselves. After you've come through on the other side and can look back, though, it's a whole different story.

Another little tidbit from the treasure trove of Peggy Benson: Take a piece of notebook paper and make two columns; one you call *Good things in my life,* and the other *Bad things in my life.* Given time, Peggy says, you'll be able to move items from the bad side to the good side. Those huggermuggers that cause us the most pain are often the very things that make us strong, give us character, and cause us to know God in a new and real way. Sometimes these bad things that happen to us can give us a new point of view, a new lease on life, and give us a deeper love and appreciation for friends and loved ones. It was true for me.

Eighteen years ago I had cancer, and my prognosis (in simple, nonmedical terms) was, *You'll be dead soon!* To make a long story short, I'm not dead! I'm here! Was cancer a *bad thing?* Was chemotherapy horrendous? Yes and yes again! But wait? Was it a *good thing?* Yes to that too! It changed my heart and it changed my life. The journal I kept during that very difficult time became a book (*I'm Alive and the Doctor's Dead*), which led to other books, speaking engagements, and the incredible opportunity to meet lots of new people, which is my goal in life: *to meet lotsa people!*

Not only did I have breast cancer, but eighteen years later my daughter Dana was diagnosed with the disease. The day Wayne and I got the news was possibly the worst day of our lives. We were completely wiped out. I remember feeling as though my body was made of jelly. A cowering, quivering blob of jelly! I'm sure Wayne felt the same way, but knowing my husband as I do (and knowing he's typical of the male species), his mind was busy trying to figure out how to fix it!

We were just kind of huddled in our state of numbness, staring into space, when the phone rang. My mind and body knew what to do only because of years of conditioning: answer it! It was our friend Mark Lowry, and either from osmosis or from the grapevine, he knew about Dana.

"I'm picking you up in twenty minutes," he said firmly. "My mom and dad are here. We'll go to Murfreesboro for Mexican food. We can talk on the way."

"Wait, let me check with Wayne," I responded. I was in a daze, not wanting to shake myself from my stupor, much less eat Mexican food.

"*Tell* Wayne, don't ask him," was the reply. It was followed by the dial tone.

Again, conditioning kicks in. You comb your hair, change your clothes, answer the door, greet your friends, and go through the motions. After the night is over, you barely remember a thing. Yet, two years later (Dana is cancer-free and back to her old energetic self after surgery and chemotherapy), I can remember every single detail of the evening, practically down to the bumps in the road, the over-powering smells and the too-pungent taste of the food, the mockingly vivid colors of the restaurant, and sounds much too loud and far too joyous. I remember who sat where and who said what to whom.

Mark has a tendency to ask a lot of questions. Information is everything, to the point we sometimes call him *an information junkie*. That same thing could be said of my husband, and that night Wayne seemed to take comfort in Mark's questions and speculations regarding our daughter's illness. Mark's dad, Charles, never gets much publicity. He doesn't mind one bit that Mark and Bev (Mark's mother) are the celebrities in the family. They call him *the backbone of the family*. He's quiet, thoughtful, and well-spoken—a lawyer, for heaven's sake! Sitting around the table that night, it was almost as if this threesome could solve not only the dilemma at hand, but any other crisis as well, given enough discussion.

Bev (a talented writer and singer in her own right) is an answer person. She'll spit out a solution practically before the question is framed. She knows! She's a bona fide psychology professor, having gotten her degree long after her children were grown. Even though she possesses *book knowledge,* it's her *heart knowledge* that draws you to her. Her approach is simple: *God is at work. Do his will, and you can trust him for the outcome.*

Charles prayed that night, and as the song says, *Take your burden to the Lord and leave it there*—we did! I remember thinking (albeit somewhat fatalistically): *That's that! What else can we do? We either believe what we say we do, or we don't.*

Most of all, I remember feeling as though I was in a safe cocoon, surrounded by love and comfort. I knew I didn't have to talk, didn't have to be interesting or funny (even with Mark Lowry). Didn't have to *be anything!* Being a blob was okay.

In the future when I'm asked that question—if it's possible to find ways to celebrate even when you're going through tough times and feel there is nothing to celebrate— I'm ready! I'll explain about the sheet of paper with the bad and good lists, about having had cancer, and how it changed my life and heart. I'll tell about dealing with my daughter's illness, and about good friends, Mark and his parents, and the Mexican restaurant, how I felt like a blob but knew it was okay to feel that way. How Dana's experience changed her life and that of her husband; and . . . !" By now the interviewer is looking at the clock, trying to shut me up and wondering whatever happened to the sound-bite concept.

". . . So in answer to your question . . . yes, *it is possible,*" I'll say with great conviction. *"But perhaps only in retrospect!"* By this time the audience will have forgotten the question, the interviewer will be exasperated, and not a moment too soon, they'll cut to a commercial.

Chapter Forty-Two

God of the Mountain

When I'm wondering where God is in all the turmoil of life (like when my daughter had cancer), I find encouragement from music. A song that jumps out at me when I'm going through hard times is "God of the Mountain," and although it's been recorded by other people, my favorite version is by Lynda Randall. Even in the midst of this serious thought I must tell you, dear reader, about Lynda. She claims to be a total tomboy, but I can assure you that when she dresses up, she looks like a movie star! When I saw her perform on New Year's Eve she had on a Renoir-red satin pant-suit that would cause you to sin for want of it. She had a zillion little bitty braids framing her pretty brown face—like those auras that surround the heads of saints in museum paintings. I loved her "do" so much I went out and bought a "do" for myself—a *blond* hairpiece with little bitty braids! It didn't work for me like it did for Lynda. Now back to the serious!

God of the Mountain

Life is easy when you're up on the mountain,
and you've got peace of mind like you've never known:
But when things change and you're down in the valley,
Don't lose faith, for you're never alone.
We talk of faith when we're up on the mountain,
but talk comes easy when life's at its best,
But in the valley of trials and temptations,
that's when faith is really put to the test.

CHORUS
And the God on the mountain
is still God in the valley,
When things go wrong,
He'll make them right;
And the God in the good times
is still God in the bad times,
The God of the day
is still God of the night.

Copyright © 1975 by Gaviota Music, 35255 Brooten Road,
Pacific City, OR 97135. All rights reserved.
Used by permission. (BMI)

Chapter Forty-Three

Blessed Are the Desperate! Just Please God, Don't Let Me Be One of Them!

Picture yourself! Married with two children. A good wife and mother. You discover your husband is in love with another woman. You are helpless. The unthinkable happens—*You don't believe in it, for heaven's sake!*—you are divorced.

You pick yourself up and go on. Unlike other women you've known, you are fortunate to have a career in place. Even better, your career is in *ministry!* You are part of a Christian singing group that is in demand everywhere. You've won Grammy and Dove awards and "Group of the Year" twice.

Just when you think, "I'm going to be able to keep it together, feed my kids, pay the rent, and have a ministry," it's discovered that one of your group members is having an affair with a well-known Christian singer. Your career, as you know it, is over. That is what happened to my friend Bonnie Keen, a delightful young woman Wayne and I have known for years. We scheduled her as often as possible to sing on our corporate sound tracks. She was the best session singer in Nashville before forming (with two friends) the group First Call. Not only did she bring superb musical abilities, but she brought a charisma, a joie de vivre! There was also an intangible—a magical—thing happened when Bonnie was in the studio. At the end of the day you felt better just from having worked with her.

What I've told you about Bonnie, dear reader, are *just the facts*. Between the lines is gut-wrenching devastation. Bonnie's book, *Blessed are the Desperate for They Will Find Hope*, takes you on that journey.

Between the lines is grief! A *fall-on-the-floor-in-a-jelly-like-puddle* kind of grief!

Between the lines is guilt! *"If only I had . . ."* thoughts take over the days. Nightmares take over the nights.

Most devilish of all is the ". . . but *I don't believe in divorce*" factor and its twin: the horrendous "*Christians* don't believe in divorce" stigma that attaches itself like a leech to everything you were, are, and ever hoped to be. It's the reason I began this chapter by saying, "Picture yourself . . . !" We rarely do!

Here is what I know about Bonnie now—we had lunch just last week. She's still the same six-foot, blonde-haired beauty she always was. The charisma is there; the joie de vivre is there, and she still possesses a personality as dynamic as anyone I've ever known. She grabbed me, whirled me around, kissed my cheeks, prayed a blessing on me and promised to build a shrine in my honor! And that was before we entered the restaurant! But Bonnie Keene King (newly married!) is very different. She's not the same person she once was. She's been through the fire, and the fire has refined her. On the other side of the flame she's found peace.

"When I stopped to create my own definition of peace, my eyes were at last opened to a beautiful vista I had previously been blind to. And the wooing of the Lord brought me to rest in his vision for my life, to try to live accepting the grace of Christ."

God has redeemed Bonnie's past, given her a heart of compassion, and provided a unique platform (by means of her book, her

new recording projects, and her speaking engagements) for bringing hope to other women who have had like experiences.

As I travel the country, I meet young women who dream for a
career, a ministry, such as Bonnie's. To those of you who are dream-
ing I just have this to say, "Picture yourself! First of all in ministry.
Now play it backward. Is it worth it?"

Celebrate outdoors.
Circle your table with
candles or luminaries.
Use colorful dish towels
for napkins, and decorate
the table with weeds tied
with ribbons. Garden tools
make wonderful props.

Chapter Forty-Four

Even If We're Scarred for Life, We Must Preserve the Traditions

When Bonnie Keen and I are together, she always talks about her children. They are her priority. Perhaps people who live an on-the-road life work harder at parenthood than others. They have no choice but to make the moments count. While Bonnie and I were having lunch, I discovered that one of the things she works hard at, in light of the divorce, is carrying on family traditions. "Oh this is great for my book!" I said and begged her to send me something from her bag of tricks. The story she sent me by email wasn't exactly what I expected—I thought it would be a perfect little story about a perfect little tradition in her perfect little family. Instead, it was . . . what shall I say? Real life! That's it! Real life! Read it, keeping in mind you are more likely to remember (and hopefully laugh at for years to come) experiences that go wrong, than you are those that go right.

Bonnie's story:

> I love shellfish. I adore and crave anything with ocean-stained pinchers and crust that has to be peeled off—the kind of sea creatures we humans devour while leaving our fingers

shredded and our palates grateful for the small nuggets of rich, sweet meat.

I started putting plates of seafood in front of my two-year-old daughter as soon as she had enough teeth to contend with any of your basic shelled critters—broiled, baked, and soaked in butter with lemon. Courtney was two and a half when she had her first bite of lobster, and I knew the child was truly in trouble! She *loved* it and managed to eat an entire platter of Oysters Rockefeller to boot!

By the time she was three I took her to my favorite restaurant in Hilton Head, South Carolina. With a purely DNA-driven instinct, Courtney walked up to the tank that held the array of unsuspecting red-shelled delights and picked out her choice for this—ridiculously expensive, yet priceless in light of the experience—lobster dinner. "I'll have Frank! That's him, right there!" she proudly announced. "Now, you name yours!"

"I'll call mine Hal," I gulped. Poor guy! Doomed to be served at our table with his buddy Frank.

To my utter amazement, Courtney ate Frank without a show of sentiment—and in his entirety! By the time we got back to our hotel, she was sleeping soundly and satisfied to the gills (sorry) with her accomplishment.

Courtney, now seventeen, has never lost her taste for shell-fish and she shares that passion with her younger brother, Graham. (*What have I done?*) The other thing they love is pizza. Not any old pizza, but Chicago pizza!

During my single parenting years, healing from my divorce, wrestling with finances and fears, and being an abysmal failure in the dating arena, I was especially determined to keep our family traditions with food and meals as normal as possible. (When all else fails and things look bad, food can definitely be a great place to forget life and be selfish, if only for a moment.)

Traveling for so many years left me with one favorite food-related tradition. When I had to be in Chicago, I'd buy a huge, awesome REAL DEAL pizza and bring it home for dinner. When I was in Boston (or any other city known for its seafood), I'd bring lobsters. They can be packed up neatly to fit in the overhead.

"Guess what I got today on the way home?" I would say and smile smugly. The kids would know immediately it was either pizza or something with claws. This was so much fun for me and in some way soothed that need to carry on family traditions. There was a time however, and captured on video no less, when I finally crossed the line.

I'd arrived home from a concert date in Boston with three huge lobsters in a box with their pictures on the side. I was so proud of myself! I just couldn't wait to get out the boiling pot, salt, butter, the works. I had french bread and corn to go on the side. At the last minute I decided to fire up the video camera to capture the kids and me having this memorable moment together.

It just so happened that Graham, age six at the time, had never seen the actual demise of the lobsters he so loved. He'd always seen them just afterwards, steaming on a plate, looking so peaceful and ready to be eaten. Courtney, age ten, knew how the process went, but didn't seem to mind. To her the end result was worth the *meany means*.

Opening the box that held the lobsters, I called the kids in to help. I thought this would really be fun. We hadn't named them or bonded or anything yet, the pinchers were rubber banded together, and (as the man who packed them said) they were asleep, on ice and out cold, literally! As Courtney and Graham ran into the room, I turned on the camera and told them to each grab the one they liked and put it face down in the boiling water.

Courtney inched up carefully, asking if they were really asleep and gingerly picked up her lobster. Much to our horror, he was awake and not too happy about having been confined in a cold box with pinchers out of action. When he started to wiggle, Courtney started to scream and dropped him on the floor. Still filming, I worked my way over picked up another one and he too decided to fight back! I began to scream. Now two people were screaming and jumping around, and two lobsters were flailing around for dear life on the floor. Poor little Graham went wacko.

"The poor lobstuhs! The poor lobstuhs!" he cried.

I handed the camera to Courtney and tried to assure him that they were really not themselves and had no idea what was going on.

"Don't kill them, Mom! Please don't kill them!" he howled. "Does it hurt? Oh no! Oh no!"

As I'm trying to comfort my child, I'm picking up the dastardly little uncooperative critters and putting them, one by one, into the water.

"This puts them to sleep forever . . . they don't feel a thing," I'm saying. Then all of a sudden, I'm crying, and Graham is wailing, "You killed them! You killed them!" Tears are streaming down his face and mine. I'm jumping around, corralling the lobsters, and dunking them into their watery grave as fast as I can.

Courtney—by now she's crying too—never misses a Polaroid moment so to speak, and by the end of our "moment" the video tape shows us in total chaos. All of us are in tears, and I'm trying my best to make my kid believe his mother is not a cold-blooded murderer!

Things did eventually calm down, and we did actually enjoy our meal, which I was determined to see through to the finish. *Those things cost a fortune!* I never dared to bring live dinner home again. Graham is now thirteen, and believe me, we have had more than our share of fiascos, times I've tried to be the perfect mother and failed. Thankfully, all of them aren't on video! I recently released a new CD called "Marked for Life." My son insists, and perhaps he's right, it should have had a picture of him and his sister on the front, and that it should have been called "Scarred for Life."

This is a perfect example of taking something that went terribly wrong and making a wonderful and memorable story out of it. Courtney and Graham will be telling this to their children and grandchildren.

Chapter Forty-Five

Grace for the Moment? What about Tomorrow and the Next Day? What about Next Week?

You've seen Buddy Greene in concert and on TV, singing (in a hauntingly back-country voice), and playing the harmonica. Buddy doesn't play just *one* harmonica. He plays *many* harmonicas! All shapes and sizes. He has a whole duffle bag full of them, and he can take you to New Orleans via jazz, to Nashville by way of country, or down the Mississippi, blue grassin' all the way! When he does his medley of train songs, you'll be transported back in time to the era of the Wabash Cannon Ball, and you'll be hangin' on to the side of that steam engine for dear life!

Buddy and his wife, Vicki, were first friends of Bob and Joy MacKenzie, but through the years they've become our friends too. Before Bob died, when we would run into each other around town, we'd say "Isn't it about time for the MacKenzies to invite us all to dinner?"

Wayne and I have come to love Buddy and Vicki and to admire them as they lived out their Christianity by going the extra mile with Bob during his long illness. Joy would readily tell you that Buddy came just about every day he was in town, prepared to run errands, help with personal tasks, or read articles and Scripture after Bob's eyesight was gone. He never failed to pray with and for Bob. When Buddy wasn't there, Bob played his CD over and over. His favorite song—mine too! I often find myself singing it—was "Grace for the Moment." When I get sick of my own wretched voice, I play the CD.

Grace for the Moment
Buddy Greene and Trish Walker

When I fret over outcomes that I cannot see,
It's for certain I'll not have the peace meant for me,
But when with thanksgiving I just look to Him
He will answer me time and again with . . .

CHORUS
Grace for the moment, all that I need
Grace for the moment and faith to receive
The promises given to those who believe
Grace for the moment, all that I need
If I understand faith, it's not counting on me
It's the hope and assurance of what I can't see
It's the daily relying on Jesus to be
Providing more grace faithfully
Further proving His great love for me with . . .

(repeat chorus)

Used with permission Spirit Quest Music/Rufus Music & Songs of Crossfield

Chapter Forty-Six

Refining Fire . . . from Glob of Sand to Objet d'Art

O ther than the spectacular display of nature, there wasn't a lot to see in the "almost-heaven" state of West Virginia when I was a child growing up there. When we had out-of-town guests the great attraction was Hawks Nest State Park, where you could stand on a precipice high above the New River Gorge and see for miles.

Part of the adventure of going there was traveling the narrow, two-lane road that wound its way around such treacherous hairpin curves that you practically met yourself coming and going. Along the way were roadside stands, colorful with chenille bedspreads hanging from droopy clotheslines, their turkey motifs flapping in the wind. I dreamed of owning one of my own, but eventually came to realize that "over my dead body" meant it would never be so.

The picnic Mother would pack always included a couple of her homemade pies, and after we were stuffed to the gills, we would tour the museum to see the *also stuffed to the gills* eagles, mountain lions, and snakes that were indigenous to the area. There must have been other exhibits, other birds and animals displayed there, but those are the ones I was drawn to, the ones I remember.

Another *always-on-the-agenda* tourist attraction was a trip to

Blenko Glass, in the tiny town of Milton, an hour's drive west of Charleston. You've heard of *Nowhere USA?* That's Milton! Then and now! Having arrived in town, you practically have to be a detective to find the road—it's been called *the dirt road to nowhere*—that leads to Blenko. (If you look closely, you can see it may have been paved at one time—*perhaps right after the Great Depression!*)

The story of the Blenko family is fascinating in that founder William H. Blenko Jr.'s childhood intrigue with furnaces led him to a life-long passion for decorative glass. He came to America from London in the mid 1890s to produce hand-blown glass for stained glass windows. After several attempts, many failures, bankruptcies, and at least one return to England, William decided to give it one last try. He was sixty-seven years old when he moved to Milton, West Virginia, choosing that tiny town (to this day it's called *Milton on the Mud!*), if for no other reason than the plentiful supply of natural gas and access to the railroad. Instead of bringing in outsiders, William taught the residents the glass-blowing process. The rest is history. Today, Richard, a fourth generation Blenko, is at the helm of this world-renowned company.

The aesthetics of the place hasn't changed much at all over the years. Even after you've parked in the dirt lot, you keep wondering if you're really there. Chances are, you've missed the tiny sign, and it's hard to believe the huddle of shack-like buildings—just a cut above the old barnyard lean-to—could be the source of art glass sold in *la-de-da galleries* all over the world.

When I was a child, I loved the visitors' tour which was nothing more than moving at your own pace along a wooden walkway—a sort of indoor-outdoor kind of arrangement—that allowed you to follow the glass-making process from searing blob to finished *objet d'art.* Vases of all shapes, sizes, and colors! Pitchers, compotes, candy dishes, platters, fruit bowls, as well as decorative fruit and glass spheres to go in them.

I could have hung over those rails forever, with the heat of the ovens burning my face to almost sunburn proportions. Mesmerized! As those magnificent artisans—disguised as workmen in singed, stained, and tattered overalls—danced the dance of the refining process to the deafening music of the glowing ovens. As though a spell had been cast over me, I would inch my way along the bar on my tippy-toes, not missing a single motion.

From blob on the end of a long pipe, to fiery oven, to the baili-wick of a master craftsman who with great skill—and with such force that his cheeks looked as though they would explode—blew shape into the nothingness. With long wooden paddle in hand, a second workman (dance partner if you will) would dart in and out and around the fiery mass with such precision that at times it seemed like one finely-tuned apparatus. Shaping! Turning! Spinning! Trimming! Fluting! In and out of that hellish furnace. Burning. Searing. Making beautiful!

I learned early on that no two pieces of hand-blown glass are alike. Each one has it's own unique identity. Often an anomaly will become the very thing that sets it apart and gives it value. I devoured the pamphlets and books that told how the different col-ors are created, becoming especially caught up in how ruby-red glass is made.

The story goes that for centuries, since Egyptian times, artisans had tried to perfect this highly-valued glass. Other hues were cre-ated comparatively easily when substances such as magnesium or cobalt were added. Not the illusive ruby-red! Eventually, after years of being obsessed by this mystery, William Blenko Jr. uncov-ered the secret. It wasn't some chemical, not some special dye or paint, it was *sensitivity to heat!* The secret was in the heating process itself. At that moment of discovery Mr. Blenko is said to have pro-claimed, "Eureka. I've found it!"

When Wayne and I married, our Blenko glass wedding gifts

were proudly displayed on our Danish modern coffee table in our tiny garden (basement) apartment in Whiting, Indiana, and later in our first home in Wheaton, Illinois. Not long after the move, we learned it was fashionable to visit the Chicago Art Museum. *Fashionable, and* an inexpensive way to spend a Saturday afternoon! (We are still members, but the price of admission now includes plane tickets from Nashville, dinner, and a hotel room!) From the first, we were drawn to the magnificence of art glass. In the mid-seventies, when a Tiffany exhibit was unveiled we were enthralled, and found ourselves going back time after time.

Louis Comfort Tiffany! His work surpassed, in both quality and quantity, any that had preceded it! And to think his family was famous for their dealings in silver and fine jewels! Can't you just hear the insouciant young Louie saying to his father, "No, I'm not really interested in diamonds, or emeralds, or amethysts, or rubies. If you don't mind, I think I'll just chip up some glass and make lamps shades!" Can you imagine his father's response?

Of course he was so much more than a designer of intricate mosaic lamps, he was the most eclectic of artists. Tiffany was a master of vases, enamels, ceramics, and jewelry! He was a painter, an interior architect, decorator, and designer! The most celebrated of his creations, however, were his stained glass windows. His approach to them was so very sensory and he drew his inspiration from nature—insects, birds, landscapes, and flowers (he and Gloria could have gone into business together!).

Falling in love with the Tiffany windows eventually led me full circle to find that some of the most glorious of stained glass windows were created in *Milton on the Mud!* I knew nothing of this growing up, but Blenko windows grace such renowned structures as Rockefeller Center, St. Patrick's Cathedral, St. John the Divine, Liverpool Cathedral, and the Washington Cathedral. These discoveries led me to another designer of stained glass windows, Marc

Chagall—and a whole other perspective. That of funk and flamboyance!

I can't possibly visit the Art Museum in Chicago without making my way past the Tang dynasty Buddha-like sculptures (who, if the sign is true, *guide us to salvation),* through the hall of arms and armor (with such treasures as triple-barreled turnover flintlock fowling pistols from the 1650s), past the priceless silk vests embellished with jewels and worn by bishops and priests in the eighth century, to sit on the bench before the magnificent Chagall window.

On my last trip to Chicago I went straight from the soothing Tiffany angels of Second Presbyterian Church, to Marc Chagall's topsy-turvy floating figures world at the Art Institute. Chagall claimed to prefer a life of surprises, and his work shows it!

This year when I wasn't writing this book, I was reading books about glass. Both pursuits became a passion. Little did I know God had a master plan that would bring the two of them together before the book was finished. It's this simple: The friends I've talked about in this book—whom I know, without a doubt, have a party goin' on in their hearts—have been through the fire. It's as simple as that. They've danced the dance of the refining process to the deafening music of the glowing ovens.

At one point in her life, when she was in a mental institution, Sheila Walsh said: "I am dying; it is dark. God, where are you? Have you forgotten me so quickly?"

Have Bill and Gloria Gaither been through the fire? Would it be possible to write *Because he lives, I can face tomorrow,* had you not experienced the heat?

Liz Curtis Higgs once said that while most people feared getting too close to the fire—the pit of hell—she just walked right up to it and inhaled the fumes! At one time her path was so destructive, she received a dire warning to clean up her act from none other than scum-of-the-earth Howard Stern! Has Liz been through the fire?

Has Joni Eareckson been to hell and back? Has she languished in the searing embers for days on end trying to make sense of the whys and wherefores of her horrific accident?

Would Mark Lowry and his family have a clue as to how to comfort and give hope to others had they not been in desperate need of comfort and hope themselves?

A dead giveaway to what Bonnie Keen has been through is the title of her book: *Blessed are the Desperate for they will Find Hope.*

Make no doubt about it! The Master Artisan has been at work. Shaping! Turning! Spinning! Trimming! Fluting! In and out of that hellish furnace. Burning! Searing! Making beautiful! His touch has been upon these my friends. Each one is, without a doubt, *a Sothebys-Christies-Buckingham Palace-White House-L'ourve objet d'art!*

Here's the clincher! *It's the heat that has made them who and what they are in him. Thankfully, it's the anomalies that give them greater value in serving him!* To quote Mr. Blenko: "Eureka. I've found it!" It IS the heat!

Refining Fire

I've been broken down
And I've been beaten up
I'm carrying this cross
And drinking from your cup

I'm holding on in heat
That burns away desire
I'm walking through refining fire

You're washing white the stains
To bring me to your throne
You're drawing out my will

To fill me with your own
Though It's not always easy
The mandates and the mire
I'll walk through your refining fire

I know it's worth the pain
I know it's worth the price
So lead me through the flame
I'll make the sacrifice
And I will wrestle angels
If that's what you require
I'll walk through Your refining fire

Tag:
I'm dying to myself
Cause that's what you require
I'll walk through Your refining fire

Words and Music by Suzanne Jennings & Michael Sykes
Used by permission.

$\mathcal{D}$on't speak of death as something horrible. For the believer it should be a pleasant thought, like looking forward to a party. Heaven will be the greatest celebration of all. Think of it that way! Talk about it that way!

Chapter Forty-Seven

The Party's Over (So Long— Goodbye—Let's Get This Mess Cleaned up and Get Out of Here!) OR IS IT?

I have this idea I'm working on for my boys for Christmas," Lois Bock said, as we sat down to breakfast. "I want you to do something for me."

Eeek! What's she gonna ask? I'm thinking. Lois is one of those got-it-all-together, nothin'-but-the-best kind of girls. What could I possibly do for her?

"I'm asking my friends to write brief essays on what they think heaven is like. Then I'll organize them and bind them into a book for Jonathan, Steven, and Kelly (Jon's wife). It will be their Christmas gift. Will you write something for me?"

It stands to reason she's thinking about heaven these days. Fred's there, was the next thought that darted through my mind. It had been barely a year since Fred, prolific music composer and arranger, publisher and owner of Fred Bock Music, choral director at Hollywood Presbyterian Church, organist of great renown, and Lois's husband of many years, had moved to his final residence. He was transported via a medical fiasco that should never have happened—the kind you hear about on *20/20*.

Fred and Lois were known throughout the music industry for

their hospitality. They entertained like no others. So much so, that when groups of us got together *without the Bocks,* we'd joke about our own inadequacies in comparison. If a dinner or party was done well, the compliment would be "Lois Bock couldn't have done better." If something went awry it was, "That would never happen at the Bocks!" If by chance we'd put out the peanut butter jar, which we do on occasion, we'd say, "It's a good thing Fred and Lois aren't here." Some of my best recipes have come from Lois, but I could never begin to serve them in the gracious manner she does.

We were not ready to relinquish Fred and certainly not in the manner in which he went. In the process of being treated for kidney stones an artery was severed, and every system you hope is in place in the hospital to handle a major medical crisis wasn't. All the signs of trauma, and yes, even impending death, were ignored or missed at best. The bad news is, *Fred died.* The only possible good news we could think of was, *Fred became a citizen of heaven!*

Lois had been left with a million questions. Instead of sweeping her feelings under a rug and saying "Oh, it must have been God's will" (although in her heart she knew that to be true) like others might have done, Lois freely displayed her tortured psyche for all to see, and honestly shared her anguish as she tried to make sense of it all.

Lois's request got me thinking about heaven. In reflecting on her tragedy, I couldn't help but wonder why in the world we work so hard to stay alive and keep our loved ones alive long after hope is gone, if heaven truly is a place of eternal bliss—the ultimate party, for heaven's sake! Isn't it ironic that we (and notice that I'm including myself here) insist on being hooked to an octopus-like network of machines with tubes forced into our every orifice—breathing for us, cleansing our livers *and gizzards,* pushing our blood through our veins, and forcing our heart to beat—making us nothing short of robots! Isn't it stranger still, that we eagerly accept medication after medication, chemical after chemical (often one to counteract the other) and most of the time *we don't even ask why?*

When that doesn't work, we scream in God's face begging him to do a miracle, and promise unreasonable and un-do-able penance in return. If that weren't enough, we remind God how powerful he is and demand that he intervene! *Demand, mind you!*

I'm not saying I wouldn't use every means possible to prolong my own life or the lives of my loved ones. When the time comes, I'll probably be screaming at God louder than anyone, and be making demands of all sort. I don't know. I'm just saying, *what's wrong with this picture?*

The truth of the matter is, *we are fearful of the unknown,* and we tremble at the things we don't totally comprehend, not to mention the fact we don't like losing the people we love!

Knowing that most of Lois's friends would write serious pieces about heaven, I couldn't resist taking the humorous route. I adapted something I'd written in *Duh-votions* that depicts heaven as a pretty appealing place.

Here is my story for Lois and for you:

When I Think about Heaven, I Think about All the Fancy Stuff!

The twelve gates were twelve pearls, each gate made of a single pearl. The great street of the city was of pure gold, like transparent glass. Revelation 21:27.

Most people I know say they could care less about all the fancy stuff heaven has to offer, they just want to be with the Lord. Not me! Wait! *I don't mean I don't want to be with the Lord,* I just mean I really like the idea of all that fancy stuff!

Ever since I was a little bitty girl, I've liked the fancy stuff. Everyone who knows me knows that I've never gotten over being Mrs. Vandertweezers, the name I gave myself as a child when I would dress up in fancy clothes—big hat with a veil, high-heeled shoes, lotsa jewelry, long gloves, and an animal around my neck that bit it's own tail—and walk around the neighborhood. I'd dress my cat, Smokey the Pirate Don Derk of Don Day in doll clothes, lay him on his back in the doll carriage, and off we'd go. Oh, I loved the fancy stuff! Then and now!

I've heard preachers preach whole sermons on the fact our minds can't begin to comprehend how magnificent heaven will be, that our mortal minds just can't handle it. Well, I don't want to brag, *but mine can!* I can just picture me in my big ol' crown.

If you've ever watched Miss America, you know it's not easy walking with a crown on your head. I've already practiced my crown-wearing. I have a gold plastic one, with fake jewels, that I bought when my nieces, Cara and Kirby, were little girls. I would put it on and say "I'm the queen of everything and you *will* do exactly as I say." Even though they are now teenagers, I still do my act and they pretend to enjoy it. Perhaps *tolerate* is a better word!

I can picture those gates made from humongous pearls, and streets so bright you have to put on your movie-star-sized sunglasses before you take a walk. I can see myself walking up and down those streets of gold talking to all my friends—the very same friends who said they didn't care about all the fancy stuff when they were on earth, but are really *getting into it* now that they are in heaven.

Heaven is a real place. A place to look forward to, to contemplate. To prepare for! As the song says, "Wait Till You See Me in My New Home!" The beauty of it will be beyond our wildest imagination, those we've loved and longed to see will be there, all we could desire or hope for will be provided, and we'll be with our Lord. Sounds like a party to me! Strike up the band, Fred!

Dear God: Thank you that life's not over when we die; that you have prepared this incredible place to look forward to. I want to be ready. I want to be right with you. Let me show the way to others by the way I live. I, for one, am glad heaven is full of all that fancy stuff. Don't hold back! Amen.

Adapted from *Duh-votions*, by Sue Buchanan. Used with permission.